Charles Dickens

This i

Pleas

_____

_____

_____

_____

_____

_____

D1322268

Writers' Lives

Concise, accessible introductions to major writers focusing equally on their life and works. Written in a lively style to appeal to both students and readers, books in the series are ideal guides to authors and their writers.

Other titles in the series:
George Eliot: A Critic's Biography Barbara Hardy

Charles Dickens

DONALD HAWES

continuum

Continuum
The Tower Building
11 York Road
London SE1 7NX

80 Maiden Lane
Suite 704
New York, NY 10038

© Donald Hawes 2007

All rights reserved. No part of this publication may be reproduced or transmitted in any
form or by any means, electronic or mechanical, including photocopying, recording, or
any information storage or retrieval system, without prior permission in writing from the
publishers. Donald Hawes has asserted his right under the Copyright, Designs and Patents
Act, 1988, to be identified as Author of this work.

British Library Cataloguing-in-Publication-Data
A catalogue record for this book is available from the British Library.

ISBN-10: HB: 0-8264-8963-X
          PB: 0-8264-8964-8
ISBN-13: HB: 978-08264-8963-0
          PB: 978-08264-8964-7

Library of Congress Cataloging-in-Publication Data
A catalog record for this book is available from the Library of Congress.

Typeset by Fakenham Photosetting Limited, Fakenham, Norfolk

Printed and bound in Great Britain by MPG Books Ltd, Bodmin, Cornwall

BATH SPA UNIVERSITY
NEWTON PARK LIBRARY

Class No. 823.8 DIC H

Phil Dutch 20|9|07

Contents

Abbreviations and References

ACC	*A Christmas Carol*
ATTC	*A Tale of Two Cities*
BH	*Bleak House*
BR	*Barnaby Rudge*
DC	*David Copperfield*
DS	*Dombey and Son*
GE	*Great Expectations*
HT	*Hard Times*
LD	*Little Dorrit*
Letters	Pilgrim edition of Dickens's letters in 12 volumes. See under House, Storey, Tillotson *et al.* in the Bibliography.
MC	*Martin Chuzzlewit*
MED	*The Mystery of Edwin Drood*
NN	*Nicholas Nickleby*
OCS	*The Old Curiosity Shop*
OMF	*Our Mutual Friend*
PP	*Pickwick Papers*

The references in parentheses in the text of this book to Dickens's novels and to John Forster's *Life of Dickens* are to Parts and Chapters since different editions exist with different page numbers.

Introduction

This book is a guide and companion to Dickens's work, with the emphasis on his fiction. It opens with an account of the reasons for his perennial appeal. The first part of the guide consists of a brief biography outlining the main events of Dickens's personal and public life and highlighting aspects of his striking personality. The second component of the guide is a series of summaries of the novels in chronological order, with indications of critical opinion, dispersed in groups throughout the main text. The companion is wide-ranging, beginning with an account of London in reality and in Dickens's writing, since London was the urban setting that Dickens knew intimately and that was present throughout his work. After that, we turn to social class, a topic that consciously and unconsciously affected the lives of every Victorian in actuality and in fiction and that frequently excited comment and controversy. We consider crime, education and medicine and questions of their administration, which were sometimes associated with London and the class system and which were present in Dickens's mind all his life, whether he was writing fiction or non-fiction, making speeches or expressing his opinions in letters.

Narrowing the focus, we look at his presentation of women, children and animals, whether realistic, imaginative or both. The degree of personal influence and involvement is a vexed question, but we can surely suggest that this presentation is sometimes based, at various removes, on his own experience of his fellow human beings and of the animals that fascinated him. The section that deals with fictional comic characters and villains can be profitably considered in conjunction with the section that follows it: the world of entertainment. That world can incorporate Christmas celebrations, so central to what we can vaguely call Dickens's philosophy of life: Dickens and Christmas is an inescapable topic in an account of his life and work. Still on the subject of entertainment, we have to remember that public readings were popular in Victorian times, with

Dickens as their most famous performer, and so these are described in another section. Performance was an integral part of Dickens's life and writings.

A concise companion like this cannot fully place Dickens in the context of Victorian literature but it is possible to describe, under the heading of 'Friends and Contemporaries', some of the contributions made to his life and work by the contemporaries he knew best. Dickens's books, more than those of any other English novelist, have inspired adaptations and versions in every medium, and accounts of some of these testimonies to his creative genius complete this book.

I hope that this selective guide and companion will justify the reasons given at the outset for reading Dickens, but nothing you will read here approaches the real thing: the inexhaustible riches that are ours to explore in his writings.

Chapter One
Why We Read Dickens

Dickens ranks with Shakespeare as the most widely read English author. Try Google on a computer and you will find 18 million references. Preferences among his novels have varied over the years, and critical opinion of them has fluctuated. But his fiction has seldom or never been out of print. Thousands of biographies and studies have been published. Adaptations on the stage, screen, radio and television continue to proliferate. Societies devoted to Dickens flourish in many parts of the world. Gamp, Micawberish, Podsnappery and Scrooge are words to be found in standard dictionaries. The 'common reader' (in Dr Johnson's phrase) and the literary scholar find him endlessly rewarding, though in different ways.

Dickens's contemporaries had no doubts why they read him. To begin with, he made them laugh as no other writer had done. The 1830s and 1840s, when Dickens first took the world by storm, were full of comic writers – Thomas Hood, R.H. Barham, Surtees, Thackeray, Theodore Hook and the contributors to *Punch* – but he reigned supreme. Readers had never before encountered in fiction such inventive and imaginative comic episodes and characters as appeared in the *Pickwick Papers, Oliver Twist, Nicholas Nickleby* and *Martin Chuzzlewit. Pickwick Papers* bowled everybody over. An army officer, Edward Bruce Hamley, in an article that appeared in *Blackwood's Magazine* in April 1857 recalled that before *Pickwick* the world seemed a serious place until Dickens's humour 'burst forth in a genial irresistible flood, sweeping down all restraints of primness and Puritanism.' He remembered as a boy unsuccessfully trying to repress his laughter in a cathedral when he thought of Tony Weller and having to be escorted outside, where he sat on a tombstone and gave 'full vent' to his mirth (Hamley, 1857, p. 491). Thomas Arnold, the Headmaster of Rugby, in a letter of 6 July 1839 to the Reverend G. Cornish, attributed the increasing 'childishness' of boys to the 'great number of exciting books of amusement' that included *Pickwick Papers* and *Nicholas Nickleby* (Stanley, 1893, p. 355). Mary Russell Mitford, the author of *Our Village*, wrote to a Miss Jephson on 30 June 1837 that it wasn't only the boys and girls who 'talk his [Boz's] fun' but distinguished public figures as well: 'Lord Denman studies *Pickwick* on the bench while the jury are deliberating' (Collins, 1971, pp. 35–36).

But Dickens also made them weep. The deaths of Little Nell, Paul Dombey and Dora Copperfield, the pathetic plight of Dick (the pauper child in *Oliver Twist*) and Tiny Tim moved many to tears. Thackeray threw down a copy of the latest instalment of *Dombey and Son* in front of Mark Lemon, the editor of *Punch*: 'There's no writing against such power as this – One has no chance! Read that chapter describing young Paul's death: it is unsurpassed – it is stupendous!' (Johnson, 1952, p. 611). Terror could accompany the laughter and tears, as readers discovered early on with Bill Sikes's murder of Nancy and the grotesque antics of Quilp. Underlying the fascinations of Dickens's narrative was his concern for social and human improvement, sometimes expressed in the form of exposure of hypocrisy and corruption, and at other times embodied in moving portrayals of wretchedly deprived people. Dean Stanley, in his funeral sermon in Westminster Abbey on 19 June 1870 spoke of the compassion that Dickens evoked: 'He laboured to tell us all, in new, very new, words, the old, old story, that there is, even in the worst, a capacity for goodness, a soul worth redeeming, worth reclaiming, worth regenerating' (Collins, 1971, p. 525).

We read Dickens today for virtually the same basic reasons but look at them from different viewpoints because (to make an obvious statement) we are living in a different cultural world. We have experienced the fiction of Henry James, Proust and Lawrence and the artistic movements we vaguely call modernist. Brevity, cynicism and a distrust of large gestures and confident generalizations prevail. Returning to the topic of comedy, we can still appreciate, but perhaps to a less extent, Dickens's geniality and warm-heartedness in the Christmas scenes at Dingley Dell and in his portrayal of Joe Gargery and R.W. Wilfer. But we have no reservations about his comedy when it is cruel or sardonic, as in some of Sam Weller's similes or in the scene in *Nicholas Nickleby* where Mrs Squeers is dosing the boys with brimstone and treacle, 'choking the last boy in her hurry, and tapping the crown of his head with the wooden spoon to restore him' and then calling up 'a little boy with a curly head' so that she can wipe her hands on it (NN, ch. 8). Mrs Skewton, a woman of artifice through and through assures Mr Dombey that Nature intended her for an Arcadian: 'I am thrown away in society. Cows are my passion. What I have sighed for, has been to retreat to a Swiss farm, and live entirely surrounded by cows – and china' (DS, ch. 21). Mr Podsnap corrects the French guest's pronunciation of English and dismisses the outside world of foreigners: 'with his favourite right-arm flourish, he put the rest of Europe and the whole of Asia, Africa, and America nowhere' (OMF, ch. 11). The unexpected details are comically apt: the curly head Mrs Squeers wipes her hands on, the cows and china in surrealistic juxtaposition, the right-arm gesture. All told, Dickens's comedy is as wide-ranging and as varied in mood as Shakespeare's.

Dickens's presentation of pathos is controversial. We are suspicious of sweet or noble expressions of melancholy or of elevating deathbed scenes, though such feelings and such scenes were grounded in fact. Common causes of complaint are that children like Oliver Twist or Tiny Tim are impossibly virtuous and precocious and that Dickens's language becomes inflated and falsely rhythmical and figurative in scenes like his description of Little Nell's death, written practically as blank verse. Even so, it is fair to assume that more people today are moved by such characters and events than are prepared to admit it. Sometimes the pathos has the ring of sincerity. The death of Mr Dombey's first wife in childbirth in the first chapter of *Dombey and Son* gains its poignancy from the complex of emotions of which it is a part; it is one strand of a chapter that subtly introduces us to themes of pride, heartlessness and filial love. Its last sentence is echoed in variations of sea imagery later in the novel: 'Thus, clinging fast to that slight spar within her arms, the mother drifted out upon the dark and unknown sea that rolls round all the world.' Then there are Mrs Gradgrind's dying words in *Hard Times*: 'I think there's a pain somewhere in the room … but I couldn't possibly say that I have got it' (HT, II, ch. 9). Or consider Bella's visit in *Our Mutual Friend* to her father's office, where she sees that his desk is the shabbiest in the room and indignantly learns from him that it's called 'Rumty's Perch': 'You see, being rather high and up two steps, they call it a Perch. And they call *me* Rumty.' The poor, affectionate clerk typically excuses them, despite her anger at their behaviour: 'They're playful, Bella, my dear; they're playful' (OMF, III, ch. 16). It's the same kind of sadness that earlier marked Dickens's picture of the Cratchits, made all the more touching by the smile that accompanies it.

We can still agree without reservation that Dickens has the power to excite and terrify (sometimes horrify) his readers. Bill Sikes's murder of Nancy in *Oliver Twist*; the riots and bloodshed in *Barnaby Rudge* and *A Tale of Two Cities*; the opening scene on the marshes when Pip meets the convict in *Great Expectations*; the storm at Yarmouth in *David Copperfield*, when Steerforth and Ham are drowned; Merdle's suicide by cutting his jugular vein in a great marble bath in *Little Dorrit*; and Krook's death by 'spontaneous combustion' in *Bleak House*. Dickens uses all kinds of means to represent these episodes: exuberant prose to render the Gordon Riots, a loathsome but vague description of Krook's remains and child's eye evocations of Pip's fears. After Merdle's suicide, we realize how like a *danse macabre* was Fanny's last sight of him just after he had borrowed a penknife: 'Waters of vexation filled her eyes; and they had the effect of making the famous Mr Merdle, in going down the street, appear to leap, and waltz, and gyrate, as if he were possessed by several Devils' (LD, II, ch. 24).

Dickens's exposure of certain social ills and anomalies still has an historical interest and importance: the plight of the poor in the workhouses and slums, the lack of urban sanitation, the absurdities and delays of legal proceedings, the incompetence and obstructiveness of the Circumlocution Office and the force-feeding of facts in schools. Abuses akin to these still exist and we may still find lessons to learn from them, as the Marxist critic, T.A. Jackson, maintained in his *Charles Dickens: The Progress of a Radical* (1937). Other commentators, in Dickens's own time and in ours, have found his attitude vague, sentimental and ill-informed. In an article in the *Observer* on 23 December 1979 (that is, in the Christmas season), Conor Cruise O'Brien, the political and literary critic, maintained that Dickens helped 'to establish a certain intellectual and moral climate: a foggy climate' and that the French regard such a climate 'with cynical contempt'. O'Brien would like his children 'to respect Balzac, but prefer Dickens, although [he realized] that this preference will befog their intellects and endanger their economic prospects'. But when all is said and done, Dickens's fundamental moral teaching is of the utmost value. It is, as Michael Slater asserts in his *An Intelligent Person's Guide to Dickens*, a 'grand and urgent concern with human brotherhood and sisterhood, with mutual kindness, benevolence, justice and freedom' (Slater, 1999, p. 29). We need only to point to the enduring popularity of *A Christmas Carol*, the most frequently printed and performed of Dickens's works, to appreciate the enduring relevance of his message. The worth of human love has seldom been more movingly expressed than in the last sentence of *Little Dorrit*. Arthur Clennam and Little Dorrit leave the church after their wedding: 'They went quietly down into the roaring streets, inseparable and blessed; and as they passed along in sunshine and shade, the noisy and the eager, and the arrogant and the froward and the vain, fretted, and chafed, and made their usual uproar' (LD, II, ch. 34).

Most people read Dickens to make contact with the literally thousands of characters that he created – George Newlin in his *Everyone in Dickens* calculates that there are '3,592 name usages, and nearly that many named characters' (Newlin, 1995, I, p. xx). Arguments have forever gone on about the reality or unreality of these, but faced with so many fictional personages generalizations are impossible. Some are exaggerated embodiments of human qualities: virtue (Agnes Wickfield), flirtatiousness (Dolly Varden), meanness (Scrooge), hypocrisy (Pecksniff) and pride (Mr Dombey). Others are macabre or monstrous, like Quilp and Dennis, the hangman. Dickens is more subtle in his portrayals of those faced with dilemmas, disappointment and frustration: Rosa Dartle, Lizzie Hexam, Bradley Headstone, Miss Wade and Louisa Gradgrind. He uses some characters in order to satirize social privilege, misused wealth, maladministration and the law, and others (especially children and the poor) to arouse our compassion. For many readers, the comic characters are the favourites: Sam Weller, Vincent Crummles, Mrs Gamp, Mr Micawber, Mr Wemmick and Mrs Wilfer. All of them spring to life as soon as we meet them, visually and orally. When Ralph Nickleby first sees Mr Mantalini, he is 'dressed in a gorgeous morning gown, with a waistcoat and Turkish trousers of the same pattern, a pink silk neckerchief, and bright green slippers, and had a very copious watch-chain wound round his body. Moreover, he had whiskers and a moustache, both dyed black and gracefully curled' (NN, ch. 10). Mr Pancks, in *Little Dorrit*, 'had dirty hands and dirty broken nails, and looked as if he had been in the coals; he was in a perspiration, and snorted and sniffed and puffed and blew, like a little labouring steam-engine' (LD, I, ch. 13). When David Copperfield says that he supposes Uriah Heep to be 'quite a great lawyer', Heep's reply gives us straightaway the key to his nature: ' "Me, Master Copperfield?" said Uriah. "Oh, no! I'm a very umble person"' (DC, ch. 16). We do not need external evidence that Dickens saw and heard his characters as presences that seized hold of his imagination, but we have such evidence in his daughter Mamie's recollection of seeing him enacting them in front of a looking-glass when busy writing about them, in his pacing the streets before he got down to describing the death of little Paul Dombey and in his intense involvement in his public readings (Hawes, 1998, p. 2). Another cause of dispute is his use of strange but striking names – a device as old as fiction itself. But one can hazard a guess that his choice of names, which he agonized over, is still an additional source of entertainment for his readers. The names can suggest their person-alities, either obviously like Lord Frederick Verisopht, Gradgrind and Cheeryble or less openly like Scrooge, Nandy, Skimpole, Miss Flite and Honeythunder. A number of his characters were imita-tions or transformations of people he knew – the most notorious example is Skimpole, based on Leigh Hunt. We must acknowledge the contribution made by Dickens's illustrators since our images of Fagin, Scrooge, Mr Dombey and countless others owe much to George Cruikshank, John Leech and Phiz, who worked under Dickens's attentive supervision.

These personages are realized by means of – even in terms of – Dickens's language, which provides a fundamental reason why we read him. Like Shakespeare, Dickens wrote at a time when the English language was expansive and exuberant, as we can read in sermons (widely sold in book form), political speeches (like Gladstone's), and the writings of Carlyle, Ruskin, the Brontës and Charles Kingsley, among others. Victorian architecture, painting, furniture, decor and clothes were similarly extravagant. Dickens, perhaps with some of his own early prose in mind, was aware of overindulgence in elaboration. David Copperfield, listening to Mr Micawber's verbose exposure of Uriah Heep's misdoings, observes: 'We talk about the tyranny of words, but we like to tyrannize over them too; we are fond of having a large superfluous establishment of words to wait upon us on great occasions; we think it looks important, and sounds well' (DC, ch. 52). But Dickens delighted in his own linguistic virtuosity, displayed in such passages as the visionary transformation of Scrooge's room when it is piled up with Christmas food, Carker's death under the railway train, the London fog at the beginning of *Bleak House* and the storm at Yarmouth in *David Copperfield*. If we wholeheartedly accept the amplitude of such prose (which can transfix us when read aloud with appropriate regard to intonation and rhythm), we respond with incredulous admiration to Dickens's metaphorical originality, his animation of the inanimate, his surrealistic flights of fancy and his inexhaustible invention of idiolects. Like Shakespeare again, Dickens can also write with simplicity about a moving or significant sight or action. Florence Dombey, on her wedding day, kneels in the dusty church where the sun can't penetrate: 'The morning luminary is built out, and don't shine there' (DS, ch. 57). Mrs Gargery aggressively cuts the bread: 'First with her left hand she jammed the loaf hard and fast against her bib – where it sometimes got a pin into it, and sometimes a needle, which we afterwards got into our mouths' (GE, I, ch. 2). Mrs Lammle (in *Our Mutual Friend*) is looking at her husband: 'There was a mirror on the wall before them, and her eyes just caught him smirking in it' (OMF, II, ch. 4). Dickens's non-fictional prose, in his articles in *Household Words*, *All the Year Round* and elsewhere, is never workaday journalism, since it is invariably deeply felt, records his own direct experience, and is never expressed with tiredness and cliché. No English writer displays so many varieties of prose.

Enter a Dickens novel and you enter a highly charged, multitudinous world, in which realism and imagination are interfused as never before or since. Reading the fiction can be an inspiring, moving, frightening and hilarious experience but one that once encountered and absorbed cannot be forgotten.

Chapter Two
Life of Dickens

Charles John Huffam Dickens was born at 13 Mile End Terrace, Portsea, Portsmouth, on 4 February 1812, the second child and eldest son of John and Elizabeth Dickens (who later had six more children, two of whom died in infancy). John Dickens was a clerk in the Navy pay office at Portsmouth. His duties meant that he and his family had to move to Somerset House in London in 1815 and two years later to Chatham, where Charles spent a happy few years before the family again moved to London in 1822. There they led a nomadic existence, living at first in a little house, 16 Bayham Street in Camden Town, but they were unable to settle there or anywhere else for long, since although John Dickens was still employed as a government clerk he was constantly in debt. When he was twelve Charles was sent to work at Warren's Blacking Warehouse in Hungerford Stairs, just off the Strand. His job there was the menial one of pasting labels on the bottles of blacking used in those days for boots and grates. Soon afterwards, on 20 February 1824, his father was imprisoned for debt in the Marshalsea Prison, and Charles had to live in lodgings. This traumatic period in his life was so humiliating that he spoke of it in later life only to his wife and his close friend, John Forster.

After coming to an agreement with his creditors, John Dickens was released from prison on 28 May and (against his wife's wishes) sent Charles to school at the Wellington House Academy in Hampstead Road. He left school in 1827, worked as a solicitor's clerk for a short time and in November 1828 became a newspaper reporter. He had a passionate love affair with Maria Beadnell, a banker's daughter, but this came to an unhappy end in 1833. His career as an independent writer began on 1 December 1833, when his short story, 'A Dinner at Poplar Walk' (later retitled 'Mr Minns and his Cousin'), was published in the *Monthly Magazine*.

Dickens's experiences in these twenty years, remembered and imaginatively transformed, enriched everything he wrote. There were the books that he read and reread in his Chatham days: *Robinson Crusoe*, Fielding, Smollett, *The Vicar of Wakefield* and the *Arabian Nights* were among his favourites. Other youthful reading came later in London when at eighteen he acquired a ticket for the British Museum reading room – one of the first books he ordered was an edition of Shakespeare. More potent influences were the people, scenes and things he saw, heard and felt at first hand: the noisy crowded London streets of the 1820s and 1830s, the boys who worked alongside him in the blacking warehouse (including one named Bob Fagin), prisoners in their cells in the Marshalsea, his schooldays in Chatham and London, the cases he came across in the lawyer's offices and witnessed in the courts, and the parliamentary debates and elections he reported for newspapers using his amazing skill in writing shorthand. John Forster wrote (perhaps with some exaggeration) in his biography that there was no doubt that Dickens took from the beginning of his life in Bayham Street 'his first impression of that struggling poverty which is nowhere more vividly shown than in the commoner streets of the ordinary London suburb, and which enriched his earliest writings with a freshness of original humour and quite unstudied pathos that gave them much of their sudden popularity' (Forster, I, 1).

Following the appearance of 'A Dinner at Poplar Walk', Dickens published a number of tales and sketches in the *Monthly Magazine*, the *Morning Chronicle* and other periodicals in 1834 and 1835. Their freshness, vigour and humour struck many readers with their originality. They were quickly collected in book form as *Sketches by Boz*, illustrated by George Cruikshank (a prestigious associate for such a youthful author) and published in two volumes in February 1836 (followed by a second series in 1837). Dickens used the penname 'Boz', his brother Augustus's childish attempt at pronouncing 'Moses', the nickname Charles had given him from Goldsmith's *The Vicar of Wakefield*. As a result, Dickens was known for years as 'The Inimitable Boz'. *Sketches by Boz* was a highly successful publication and, soon after the appearance of the first series, two new young publishers, Edward Chapman and William Hall, proposed to Dickens that he should write a narrative to accompany a series of engravings by the popular artist Robert Seymour depicting the adventures and misadventures of a group of Cockney sportsmen. He eagerly accepted the proposal and the result was the *Pickwick Papers*, published in monthly parts between April 1836 and November 1837. Each instalment had a green paper cover and cost one shilling (with a double instalment at the end of the run), a method of serialization that Dickens used for many of his novels in subsequent years. Seymour committed suicide after only two numbers appeared and was eventually replaced by Hablot K. Browne (calling himself 'Phiz' to match 'Boz'), a twenty-year-old artist, who thus began a long and remarkable association with Dickens. (It's worth noting that one would-be artist offering to take Seymour's place was William Makepeace Thackeray.) *Pickwick Papers* became a sensational success (especially after the introduction of Sam Weller in the fourth number), eventually selling 40,000 copies a month, and from then on Dickens became the most famous author in Britain and America. In the next five years, he wrote *Oliver Twist* (February 1837–November 1839), *Nicholas Nickleby* (April 1838–October 1839), *The Old Curiosity Shop* (April 1840–February 1841) and *Barnaby Rudge* (February–November 1841). Like all of Dickens's novels, these first came out as serials either in part-issues or in magazines. His energy and unstoppable creativity can be gauged by the fact that he was writing a number of these novels at the same time and was also writing a weekly periodical, *Master Humphrey's Clock* (1840–41), in which the *The Old Curiosity Shop* and *Barnaby Rudge* were serialized. A lover of the stage and an enthusiastic actor, Dickens wrote plays as well: *The Strange Gentleman* (1836), *The Village Coquettes*, an operetta with music by John Hullah (1836) and *Is She his Wife?* (1837) were all briefly staged in London. And as if all this productivity wasn't enough, he edited – and contributed to – *Bentley's Miscellany* (a monthly magazine), brought out an edition of the *Memoirs* of Joseph Grimaldi, the comedian (1838), and wrote (among other things) *Sunday under Three Heads* (1836, an anti-Sabbatarian pamphlet) and some humorous *Sketches of Young Gentlemen* (1838) and *Sketches of Young Couples* (1840).

On 2 April 1836, just as *Pickwick Papers* was beginning its monthly serialization, he married Catherine (Kate) Hogarth (1815–79), a daughter of George Hogarth, a prominent music critic, reviewer and editor of the *Evening Chronicle*. They lived between 1837 and 1839 at 48 Doughty Street, which is now the Charles Dickens Museum. Two of their ten children were born there. Catherine's young sister, Mary, lived with them for a few months but suddenly died at the age of seventeen on 7 May 1837, a tragic event that Dickens remembered for the rest of his life.

Between January and June 1842, he and Catherine visited the USA and Canada, landing at Boston and travelling to New York, Philadelphia, Washington, St Louis, Niagara Falls, Montreal and elsewhere. They had a rapturous welcome and Dickens made the acquaintance of many prominent Americans, including Washington Irving and Longfellow from the world of literature. But he became disillusioned about aspects of American social and political life and publicly expressed his anger at the lack of international copyright, which meant that his books could be pirated with impunity. He described his tour of the New World in a travel book, *American Notes*, published in the October of that year, a mostly factual account of his impressions. Dickens made satirical use of his experiences there in his next full-length novel, *Martin Chuzzlewit* (January 1843–July 1844), sending two of its characters, young Martin and Mark Tapley, to America for a time. Both books stirred up resentment among many American readers, who thought his depiction of their country was unjust and uninformed.

In December 1843, Dickens published the most popular of all his books, *A Christmas Carol*, illustrated by John Leech. From then on, he brought out Christmas books and stories almost every year. *The Chimes* (1844), *The Cricket on the Hearth* (1845), *The Battle of Life* (1846) and *The Haunted Man* (1848) were followed by shorter stories written in collaboration with other writers between 1850 and 1867 and published in Dickens's weekly magazines, *Household Words* and *All the Year Round*. Scrooge, the miser from *A Christmas Carol*, became a household name straightaway, to join the many other characters that had astonished and delighted Dickens's readers since 1836 with their vivid personalities and memorable sayings: Sam Weller, Fagin, Squeers, Little Nell, Dolly Varden, Pecksniff and Mrs Gamp.

Dickens began to travel widely in Europe, a practice that he continued for the rest of his life, living at various times in Italy,

Switzerland and France, relishing their languages and culture and widening his circle of friends, but never forgetting – and sometimes hankering after – the life of the London streets that unfailingly fed his imagination. *Pictures from Italy* (1846), his second travel book, illustrated by Samuel Palmer, is an account of the year he and his family spent in that country between July 1844 and July 1845, living in Genoa and Rome. For a very brief period (January–February 1846), he was the first editor of the *Daily News*, a liberal newspaper. In 1846, he privately wrote for his children 'The Children's New Testament', published in 1934 as *The Life of Our Lord*.

Dombey and Son (October 1846–April 1848), Dickens's seventh novel, marks a significant stage in his career as a novelist since it has a more unified structure and lacks some of the extravagance of the earlier fiction. It was followed by *David Copperfield* (May 1849–November 1850), which many considered (and still consider) his crowning achievement and which the novelist himself regarded as his 'favourite child'. Thanks to this book, we have been given the unforgettable characters of Mr Micawber and Uriah Heep and the most touching and lively evocation of childhood in English fiction (more memorable even than the opening chapters of George Eliot's *The Mill on the Floss*). Alongside his writing, Dickens energetically pursued other activities – speech-making, letter-writing, amateur theatricals, going for long walks, socializing and family concerns. As a man committed to philanthropic causes, he was associated with Miss Angela Burdett-Coutts (1814–1906), who used her great wealth as a member of the prominent banking family to finance various projects. He played an administrative role from 1847 onwards in the organization of one of these schemes: the establishment of Urania Cottage at Shepherd's Bush, London, as a home for the rehabilitation of 'fallen women'. As for literary matters, Dickens 'conducted' and edited *Household Words*, a weekly magazine, between 30 March 1850 and 28 May 1859, with W.H. Wills as subeditor. Costing twopence an issue, it contained fiction and non-fiction by Dickens and other contributors (whose writing was supervised and modified by him when he thought it necessary). His major publications at this time were *A Child's History of England* (serialized in *Household Words*, January 1851–December 1853), *Bleak House* (March 1852–September 1853), *Hard Times* (in

Household Words, April–August 1854) and *Little Dorrit* (December 1855–June 1857). The three last-named novels, written in times of continuing anxieties and problems in industrialized mid-Victorian England and of controversies concerning the Crimean War (which broke out in 1854), are sometimes described as 'darker' and as more seriously committed to political and social issues than the novels that preceded them.

Besides the novels of the 1850s, several crucial events occurred in the decade in Dickens's personal and professional life. After leaving the house in Doughty Street, Dickens and his family had lived in other, more upmarket London houses: Number 1, Devonshire Terrace (1839–51) near Regent's Park, and Tavistock House in Bloomsbury (1851–60). Both these houses are now demolished but the site of each has a commemorative plaque nearby. In 1856 he bought Gad's Hill Place in Kent as his principal residence, a house he had admired since his boyhood days in the area. One of his first guests was Hans Christian Andersen. Continuing his enthusiasm for the theatre, he directed – and acted in – a number of amateur productions, including Wilkie Collins's play, *The Frozen Deep*, in 1857. At the production of this play in Manchester, Dickens met and fell in love with the seventeen-year-old Ellen Ternan, who, with her mother and sister, was taking part in the play as a professional actress. He had been unhappy in his marriage for some time and this new relationship was undoubtedly a factor in his separation from his wife in May 1858. From then on, Catherine's sister, Georgina Hogarth, became his housekeeper and one of his principal confidantes. He urged Bradbury and Evans, who had been his publishers since 1844, to print in *Punch* (which they also published) his defensive account of his marital separation. When they refused to print his statement, he severed connections with the firm and in April 1859 established a new weekly magazine, *All the Year Round*, to replace *Household Words*, which Bradbury and Evans had published. Besides Dickens himself, the contributors to *All the Year Round* included Wilkie Collins, Elizabeth Gaskell and Bulwer-Lytton. In September 1857, he went on a walking tour with Wilkie Collins in the Lake District. As a result, the two of them collaborated on *The Lazy Tour of Two Idle Apprentices*, serialized in *Household Words* in October. He began a lucrative but taxing career as a public reader of his works in 1858, performing on many occasions in London and the provinces and eventually going on a reading tour of America. Dickens had always loved acting and this new supplementary profession gave him a treasured opportunity to communicate directly with an audience. His most popular readings, received with great enthusiasm, were 'A Christmas Carol', 'Bardell and Pickwick' and 'Sikes and Nancy' (from *Oliver Twist*).

Dickens wrote three more completed novels. The first two of these were *A Tale of Two Cities* (April – November 1859) and *Great Expectations* (December 1860–August 1861) which were serialized weekly in *All the Year Round*, and, like *Hard Times*, (which had been serialized weekly in *Household Words*) were therefore more concisely constructed than much of his other full-length fiction. He also published at this time two collections of sketches, essays and stories. *Reprinted Pieces*, which had originally appeared in *Household Words*, came out in 1858 as the eighth volume in the Library Edition of his works. *The Uncommercial Traveller*, consisting of some of his contributions to *All the Year Round*, was published in various editions from 1861 onwards. He returned to his use of monthly serialization in the third of his last full-length novels, *Our Mutual Friend* (May 1864–November 1865). One of his final pieces of fiction was the remarkable short story, 'George Silverman's Explanation' (in the *Atlantic Monthly*, January–March 1868 and *All the Year Round*, February 1868). After years of unremitting literary and personal activities, Dickens suffered severe strains on his health. While travelling by train on 9 June 1865 with Ellen Ternan and her mother, he was involved in a serious railway accident at Staplehurst, Kent. He escaped physical injury and was able to help other passengers in distress but the experience was traumatic. Dickens continued his programmes of public readings, including a highly successful and profitable season in America between November 1867 and April 1868, although his doctors expressed their concerns about the physical and emotional stress involved.

In 1870, Dickens began his last novel, *The Mystery of Edwin Drood*, but suddenly died of a cerebral haemorrhage at Gad's Hill Place on 9 June 1870 after writing about a half of the book, which had started to appear in monthly parts in April. Dickens had given instructions in his will that he should be privately buried but because of a general wish that he should be appropriately honoured in death he was buried on 14 June in Poets' Corner in Westminster Abbey with the minimum of ceremony. Many mourners later came to visit the grave and on Sunday 19 June the Dean of Westminster, A.P. Stanley, delivered a splendid eulogy, praising the moral and social values that Dickens had conveyed in his writings. Dickens left £93,000. His first donation in his will was £1000 to Ellen Ternan, followed by donations to his servants, members of his family and John Forster (who was joint executor with Georgina Hogarth). He wanted no 'monument, memorial, or testimonial whatever', resting his claims to remembrance on his published works, which comprise fifteen novels (one unfinished), a considerable quantity of short fiction, sketches, a few poems and plays, two travel books, a history of England and a life of Christ (both written for children), and an immense amount of journalism.

Dickens had a wide circle of friends and acquaintances, whose literary and personal relationships with him are described in a later section of this book. Everyone who knew him testified to his phenomenal energy in all that he undertook, as typified by his habit of going for long walks at a tremendous pace, sometimes through the London streets at night. Dickens was one of the leading speech-makers of his time and threw himself into literary, philanthropic and educational campaigns. He was shrewd and tough in business matters, though he also relied on the skills of Forster and other legal advisers in negotiation. He was the dominant, high-spirited figure in all gatherings and enterprises, at convivial family occasions, at public meetings and in the editorial office, ensuring efficiency and commitment from everybody. His constant mental, emotional and physical activity left its visible marks – the handsome, elegant young man of the 1830s depicted in Daniel Maclise's famous portrait (now in the National Portrait Gallery), used as a frontispiece to *Nicholas Nickleby*, had become a careworn man with a heavily lined face in the 1860s, looking far older than his years. But Forster said in his biography of Dickens that one characteristic remained the same. 'This was the quickness, keenness, and practical power, the eager, restless, energetic outlook on each several feature, that seemed to tell so little of a student or writer of books, and so much of a man of action and business in the world. Light and motion flashed from every part of it' (Forster, II, 1).

Eight of Charles and Catherine Dickens's children survived his death. Four of them made their mark in the world. Charles Culliford Boz Dickens (1837–96), their eldest son, was often in financial difficulties but continued his father's work as editor of *All the Year Round* and brought out a number of best-selling guidebooks, including a *Dictionary of London* (1879). Mary (Mamie) Dickens (1838–96), who was unmarried, always treasured her memories of her father, wrote her recollections of him in several books and edited a selection of his letters (1880–82) in collaboration with her aunt, Georgina Hogarth. Catherine (known as Kate) Macready Dickens (1839–1929) married Charles Collins (Wilkie Collins's brother) and after his death married Carlo Perugini. Both her husbands were artists and she herself was an accomplished artist who exhibited at the Royal Academy. Lucinda Hawksley's biography of her, *Katey: The Life and Loves of Dickens's Artist Daughter*, was published in 2006 (Doubleday). The most distinguished of the four was Sir Henry Fielding Dickens (1849–1933), a lawyer who became a KC and judge. Among his publications was *Memories of My Father* (1928). One of Sir Henry's granddaughters was Monica Dickens, the popular novelist of the 1940s and 1950s. Catherine Dickens, with whom Charles Dickens seldom communicated after their separation, died in 1879. Dickens's last surviving great-grandson, Cedric Dickens, died in 2006.

Chapter Three
Sketches by Boz, Pickwick Papers, Oliver Twist

Sketches by Boz (1833–37)

The *Sketches* mostly first appeared in periodicals between 1833 and 1836 and were collected in two volumes in 1836, followed by a second series in 1837, both illustrated by George Cruikshank. Dickens revised the original texts for these and subsequent editions. The subtitle explained that they were 'Illustrative of Every-Day Life and Every-Day People', for Dickens's object, as he wrote in his Preface to the first edition, was 'to present little pictures of life and manners as they really are'. They are divided into four groups: 'Our Parish', 'Scenes', 'Characters' and 'Tales'. Dickens describes scenes and people from the lower middle classes and working classes in London as they were in the middle 1830s, vividly depicting, for example, places of entertainment like 'Private Theatres', Astley's equestrian shows and Greenwich Fair and, in contrast, pathetic or forbidding places like a pawnbroker's shop and Newgate Prison. His 'Characters' include a family enjoying their Christmas dinner but also teenage prostitutes taken away in a prison van. He writes comic short stories (like 'The Bloomsbury Christening', which was immediately dramatized for the London stage) but also presents the sufferings of the destitute and social outcasts (as in 'The Black Veil' and 'The Drunkard's Death'). The contrasts in emotion, the expressions (explicit and implied) of the need for social reform and the high-spiritedness that characterize the work of Dickens are all foreshadowed in the *Sketches*.

Commentators have suggested precedents for them in the essays in periodicals by Leigh Hunt and others. But contemporary readers

were struck by Dickens's freshness and originality in his evocations of London life. In a review in March 1836, the *Metropolitan
Magazine* thought the book gave a 'perfect picture of the morals,
manners, habits of a great portion of English society' and that it was
'delightful from the abundance of its sly humour, and instructive in
every chapter' (Collins, 1971, p. 30).

Pickwick Papers (1836–37)

Dickens's sensationally successful first novel was originally called
*The Posthumous Papers of the Pickwick Club, containing a Faithful
Record of the Perambulations, Perils, Travels, Adventures and Sporting
Transactions of the Corresponding Members, edited by Boz.* Dickens
said in his Preface to the first edition in book form that his object
'was to place before the reader a constant succession of characters and
incidents; to paint them in as vivid colours as he could command;
and to render them, at the same time, life-like and amusing.' Mr
Samuel Pickwick, a middle-aged bachelor, sets out from London to
travel in various parts of England with three fellow-members of the
Club – Tracy Tupman (who is susceptible to female charms), the
'poetic' Augustus Snodgrass and the 'sporting' Nathaniel Winkle.

They were asked to forward to the Club 'authenticated accounts
of their journeys and investigations', but this aim is lost sight of as
the narrative proceeds, filled as it is with the young Dickens's high-
spirited and prolific inventiveness – there are over 150 characters.
He said himself that he abandoned the original 'machinery of
the club'. The Pickwickians, soon joined by Sam Weller as Mr
Pickwick's manservant, travel to various parts of England, where
they experience comic mishaps of every kind. Mr Pickwick in his
innocence finds himself in compromising situations with school-
girls and ladies, is taken in a wheelbarrow to the village pound as
a trespasser while sleeping off the effects of too much punch, falls
through the ice while sliding on it and so on. Mr Winkle, despite
his claims to be a sportsman, can't remount his horse and while
firing at a rook shoots Mr Tupman in the arm and so on. When Mr
Pickwick tells his landlady, Mrs Bardell, that he intends to take on
Sam Weller as his servant, she misinterprets his words as a proposal

of marriage. She sues him for breach of promise, which leads to one of the most celebrated comic scenes in English fiction: the case of Bardell v. Pickwick. Mr Pickwick loses the case and is imprisoned in the Fleet Prison. When Mrs Bardell is also imprisoned there for failing to pay her legal costs, Mr Pickwick pays them as well as the fine he has refused to pay, and so the story eventually ends happily. The outstanding character in the book is Sam Weller, whose Cockney wit, cheerfulness and resourcefulness bring aid and comfort to his master and others and have delighted generations of readers.

When the publishers Chapman and Hall commissioned Dickens to write the narrative in monthly instalments, he eagerly produced chapter after chapter with no overall plan in mind when he began. It was obvious, as he said himself, that 'no artfully woven or ingeniously complicated plot [could] with reason be expected'. The miscellaneous nature of the novel was emphasized by his inclusion of nine interpolated and independent tales of a macabre or grotesque kind. As a result, some critics have maintained that the novel is best appreciated as a sequence of entertaining events and that to approach it as one solid volume, as it were, is fundamentally mistaken. But the Bardell v. Pickwick story, begun as early as Chapter 12 and marking (as the chapter heading says) an 'epoch' in Mr Pickwick's life, is one unifying element. And his behaviour during the trial and his imprisonment shows a development in his character – the naïve and unworldly man becomes a man of principle (opposing the machinations of Dodson and Fogg, the wily lawyers) and true benevolence (helping Mrs Bardell and Mr Jingle, despite the mischief each had done him in different ways). W.H. Auden, in an influential essay, 'Dingley Dell and the Fleet', in *The Dyer's Hand* (1963) argued that the plot of the novel was essentially that of the fall of man, in that Mr Pickwick finally loses his innocence. As he made clear in later Prefaces to the novel, Dickens was aware that his contemporaries might see inconsistency in his characterization of Mr Pickwick: 'I do not think this change will appear forced or unnatural to my readers, if they will reflect that in real life the peculiarities and oddities of man who has anything whimsical about him, generally impress us first, and that it is not until we are better acquainted with him that we usually look below these superficial traits, and to know the better part of him.' Something of a fixed point in the novel after Chapter 9 is also provided by the words and activities of Sam Weller. *Pickwick Papers* is unimaginable without him as the omnipresent high-spirited but down-to-earth commentator on the ways of the world. But, above all, the novel is unified by Dickens's comic spirit (shown even in the prison scenes towards the end).

As a summary of the perennial appeal of *Pickwick Papers*, John Forster's assessment of its contemporary popularity still holds good, since he precisely lists its key characteristics: 'The charm of its gaiety and good humour, its inexhaustible fun, its riotous overflow of animal spirits, its brightness and keenness of observation, and, above all, the incomparable ease of its many varieties of enjoyment, fascinated everybody' (Forster, II, 1). Dickens briefly resurrected Sam Weller (to whom he added a son), Tony Weller (his father) and Mr Pickwick in *Master Humphrey's Clock*.

Oliver Twist (1837–39)

The original alternative title of the novel was *The Parish Boy's Progress*. Oliver Twist is born in a workhouse. His mother dies in giving birth to him and his father is unknown. Mr Bumble, the parish beadle, gives him the name of Oliver Twist. Like all the children in the workhouse, he leads a wretched, half-starved life. The boys in their desperate hunger choose him by lot to ask for more food. His famous request, 'Please, sir, I want some more', leads to his dismissal from the institution and an apprenticeship to Mr Sowerberry, an undertaker. Here he is cruelly punished for attacking Noah Claypole, who is a fellow employee, and runs away to London, where he meets the Artful Dodger, who takes him to Fagin's thieves' den. He is arrested for apparent involvement in picking the pocket of the kindly Mr Brownlow, who arranges his release from punishment and takes him into his household. But Nancy, a prostitute, and Bill Sikes, a burglar, who work for Fagin, recapture him. He gets caught while innocently taking part in a burglary of Mrs Maylie's house, but she and Rose, her adopted niece, give him comfort and refuge, just as Mr Brownlow had done. Monks, his previously unknown half-brother, in association with Fagin plots to seize him. Bill Sikes murders

Nancy, who has told Mr Brownlow and Rose of Fagin's and Monks's machinations that threaten Oliver. Trying to escape arrest, Bill Sikes accidentally hangs himself. Fagin is condemned to death. Through a series of revelations, typical of the denouement of a melodrama of the period, Oliver's parentage is revealed; he turns out to be Rose Maylie's nephew and is adopted by Mr Brownlow as his son.

The novel is remarkable for being the first to have a child as a hero throughout. In his Preface to the third edition (1841), Dickens said that he 'wished to shew, in little Oliver, the principle of Good surviving through every adverse circumstance, and triumphing at last.' Because Oliver embodies this 'principle', he is portrayed as a gentlemanly little boy who speaks educated English, however unrealistic this appears. Thackeray and others accused Dickens of sentimentalizing criminals in the manner of the popular Newgate novelists of the time – writers like Bulwer-Lytton and Harrison Ainsworth, who made heroes of their villainous protagonists. Dickens strongly rebutted the accusation. 'It appeared to me', he wrote in the same Preface

> that to draw a knot of such associates in crime as really do exist; to paint them in all their deformity, in all their wretchedness, in all the squalid poverty of their lives; to show them as they really are, for ever skulking uneasily through the dirtiest paths of life, with the great, black, ghastly gallows closing up their prospect, turn them where they may; it appeared to me that to do this, would be to attempt a something which was greatly needed, and which would be a service to society.

He maintained that he had not exaggerated Sikes's brutality or Nancy's 'redeeming traits' since he was sure that they were true characteristics of such people.

Another social purpose was his exposure of the sufferings, especially those experienced in the workhouses, caused by the administration of the Poor Laws. Kathleen Tillotson in her Introduction to the World's Classics paperback edition of the novel reminds us that Dickens has sometimes been criticized for confusing the old Poor Law and the Poor Law Amendment Act (1834) but she points out that 'he was truly reflecting conditions themselves confused' (Tillotson, 1982,

p. ix) and that a number of critics opposed or sought to amend the legislation. Besides these public issues, Dickens may be consciously or unconsciously reflecting the 'sorrows of his own childhood', as Peter Ackroyd has suggested: 'It is as if Dickens could not conceive of this fictional infant without letting loose upon him in exaggerated form all the indignities and injustices which he believed to have been heaped upon his own younger self' (Ackroyd, 1991, p. 49).

Chapter Four
Dickens's London

Dickens tells us in *Pickwick Papers* that Sam Weller's knowledge of London was 'extensive and peculiar' (PP, ch. 20) He could have equally applied those adjectives to his own knowledge of the town he had known and relished since he arrived there from Chatham when he was ten years old. London appears somewhere in all his novels, except *Hard Times*, which is set in Coketown (modelled on Preston) in the industrial north of England. E. Beresford Chancellor, in his *The London of Charles Dickens*, says in his Introduction that 'so strong was Dickens's interest in London, so invariably telling his merest references to its streets and hostels, its public buildings and its monuments, that every one of his works [except *American Notes* and *Pictures from Italy*] possesses the London air – is somehow pervaded by the metropolitan atmosphere' (Chancellor, 1924, p. 19). Dickens wrote in a uniquely vivacious fashion about its scenes and people in his first book, *Sketches by Boz*, and in many of his later pieces of journalism, collected in the *Uncommercial Traveller* and *Reprinted Pieces*. *Bleak House* begins with one isolated word: 'London'. London was present, sporadically but intensively, in his mind and imagination, whether he was living there or abroad or in Gad's Hill Place, his house in Kent. In his essay on Dickens, Walter Bagehot wrote admiringly: 'There are scarcely anywhere such pictures of London as he draws. No writer has equally comprehended the artistic material given by its extent, its congregation of different elements, its mouldiness, its brilliancy ... He describes London like a special correspondent for posterity'(Bagehot (1911), II, pp. 173–6).

John Hollingshead, a journalist who worked on *Household Words* and *All the Year Round* (and who was later a leading theatrical manager), recalled in 1900 the vital importance to Dickens's literary art of the things and people he saw in London.

His walks were always walks of observation, through parts of London that he wanted to study. His brain must have been like a photographic lens, and fully studded with 'snapshots'. The streets and the people, the houses and the roads, the cabs, the buses and the traffic, the characters in the shops and on the footways, the whole kaleidoscope of Metropolitan existence – these were the books he studied, and few others. He was a master in London, abroad he was only a workman. His foreign pictures, his American notes, his Italian sketches, were the work of a genius who could never write anything that had not striking features; but in spirit they were deficient in sympathy, and often defaced by narrow insular prejudice. (Hollingshead, 1900, p. 19)

It is unlikely that Dickens would have agreed with that last opinion but he admitted that he needed the stimulus of London life to activate his imaginative powers. Living in Genoa in 1844 and trying to write *The Chimes*, his second Christmas book, he wrote to Forster that he 'craved for the London streets' and was 'dumbfounded without his long night walks [through London]'. 'Put me down on Waterloo Bridge at eight o'clock in the evening, with leave to roam about as long as I like, and I would come home, as you know, panting to go on' (Forster, IV, 5). He made a similar complaint in a letter to Forster from Lausanne on 30 August 1846, saying that he was finding it difficult to get on with writing *Dombey and Son*, partly because of 'the absence of streets and numbers of figures. I can't express how much I want these. It seems as if they supplied something to my brain, which it cannot bear, when busy, to lose. For a week, or a fortnight I can write prodigiously in a retired place (as at Broadstairs), and a day in London sets me up again and starts me. But the toil and labour of writing, day after day, without that magic lantern, is IMMENSE!!' (Forster, V, 5).

London, the largest city in the world in the nineteenth century, had a population of almost two million in 1841, at the outset of Dickens's career. In 1871, the year after his death, this number had doubled to nearly four million. But compared to the London of today, it seems a compact city, with places like Tottenham in the north and Wimbledon in the south-west still thought of as separate villages. Although Dickens ranged all over London in his writing (and physically explored it in his phenomenal feats of walking in its streets at all times of the day), he was most familiar with areas in the north-west like Camden Town (where he lived as a boy), Holborn and Clerkenwell, with the 'legal' districts (like the Inns of Court, which he knew from his days as a lawyer's clerk), and with the City and Westminster (where he worked as a parliamentary reporter). And he was both fascinated and repelled by the wretchedly poverty-stricken and criminal areas of Seven Dials and the East End. He seldom ventures west of Charing Cross in his writing.

London was in many areas a labyrinth of narrow streets, with no system of public sanitation for most of the time that he was familiar with them. Speaking to the Metropolitan Sanitary Association on 6 February 1850, Dickens was forthright in his condemnation of the state of things: 'Of the sanitary condition of London at the present moment, he solemnly believed it would be almost impossible to speak too ill. He knew of many places in it unsurpassed in the accumulated horrors of their neglect by the dirtiest old spots in the dirtiest old towns, under the worst old governments in Europe' (Fielding, 1988, p. 106) The streets were crowded with unregulated horse-drawn traffic and were often deep in mud and droppings from horses and other animals, amounting to thousands of tons a year, which had to be cleaned by crossing-sweepers (like Jo in *Bleak House*) so that pedestrians could walk across them. Smoke from innumerable chimneys and from the newly constructed railways (as described in *Dombey and Son*) blackened buildings, faces, hands and clothes. Fog (or more precisely, smog, to use the twentieth-century word) was a persistent hazard as was the polluted Thames, which stank so badly that Parliament sometimes had to sit with the windows closed. The state of the river became particularly offensive in the summer of 1858. A year later, on 9 June 1859, *The Times* had no option 'but to assume that our metropolitan stream has at length become so thoroughly corrupted that the commonest heats of summer acting upon its surface will draw out its poison in fetid and loathsome vapours.' One of Dickens's youthful works was called *The Mudfog Papers* (1837–38), with grimly comic appropriateness. Outbreaks of cholera occurred in 1848, 1853 and 1866. Smallpox, despite the knowledge of vaccination, remained a terrible threat, as we know from *Bleak House*, in which Jo dies from the disease and

Esther's face is disfigured (although Dickens does not name the disease).

Shops and numerous business offices were small and individually owned, with their proprietors often living on the premises – clerks and other employees walked daily to the places of work, sometimes from the suburbs. In 'The Streets – Morning', one of the *Sketches by Boz*, Dickens saw 'the early clerk population of Somers and Camden Towns, Islington, and Pentonville ... pouring into the city, or directing their steps towards Chancery Lane and the Inns of Court'. Bob Cratchit, Scrooge's clerk, eagerly left the office on Christmas Eve, 'went down a slide on Cornhill ... and then ran home to Camden Town as hard as he could pelt, to play at blindman's buff (ACC, Stave 1). Clear impressions of the teeming life of the London streets can be gained by looking at Phiz's illustrations to Dickens's novels or John Leech's *Punch* drawings, where you'll see stray dogs, beggars, grinning and cheeky boys and impudent cab drivers. Even grimmer scenes were depicted by Gustave Doré in his engravings for Blanchard Jerrold's *London: A Pilgrimage* (1872). Children like Oliver Twist and little Florence Dombey could be confused and terrified in surroundings like these but others (like the young Sam Weller) learnt resilience in order to survive: Tony Weller, Sam's father, boasted to Mr Pickwick that he 'let [Sam] run in the streets when he was wery young, and shift for his-self' (PP, ch. 20). But we need not wonder that Little Dorrit was fearful when she was out at night for the first time in her life in the unlit or dimly lit streets of the capital. 'And London looks so large, so barren, and so wild,' she says to Arthur Clennam, for in her eyes 'its vastness under the black sky was awful' (LD, I, ch. 14). Mr Micawber escorted the young David Copperfield to his lodgings in Windsor Terrace, City Road, because he guessed that the boy 'might have some difficulty in penetrating the arcana of the Modern Babylon' in that direction (DC, ch. 11).

More agreeable districts existed, though Dickens portrays these less often. The rich and prosperous areas of London, including Mayfair, Belgravia and several other parts of the West End, were cleaner and more spacious. The upper classes considered an address north of Hyde Park as out of bounds. There were new buildings and monuments to be admired in the west and the south-west, including the Houses of Parliament (built 1837–60), Nelson's column (the 1840s) and Landseer's lions (1867) in Trafalgar Square, the Crystal Palace (first erected in Hyde Park in 1851 for the Great Exhibition) and the Foreign Office (1863–74). Besides Buckingham Palace there were the splendid mansions owned by the aristocracy, including Devonshire House in Piccadilly (where Dickens and his friends performed plays in the presence of the sixth Duke) and Apsley House (also in Piccadilly), the residence of the Duke of Wellington. Nevertheless, the separation between deprived districts and the more salubrious areas was not always clearly defined.

The London that Dickens first knew had changed by the time he died in 1870. The coming of the railways in the 1840s (and the first underground railway in 1863), the gradual improvements brought about after the Public Health Act of 1848, the construction of sewers between 1858 and 1875 under the supervision of Sir Joseph Bazalgette, the building of new roads (such as New Oxford Street) and less obvious brutality (public hangings were abolished in 1866) had made London a somewhat different place. Humphry House in *The Dickens World* summarized the developments in English surroundings and manners in what has become a classic formulation:'We feel that people [in *Our Mutual Friend*] use knives and forks in a different style. Everybody is more restrained ... In *Pickwick* a bad smell was a bad smell; in *Our Mutual Friend* it is a problem' (House, 1960, pp. 134–5). But the London that Dickens portrays remains predominantly the London of his younger days that had made an exciting and indelible impression upon him.

The variety of London life, with its violent contrasts between wealth and poverty, filled Dickens with ambivalent feelings of excitement, repulsion and pity. Nowhere is this complex emotional response more vitally shown than in a bravura passage of prose in *Nicholas Nickleby*:

They [Nicholas Nickleby and Smike] rattled on through the noisy, bustling, crowded streets of London, now displaying long double rows of brightly-burning lamps, dotted here and there with the chemists' glaring lights, and illuminated besides with the brilliant flood that streamed from the windows of the shops, where sparkling jewellery, silks and velvets of the richest colours, the most inviting delicacies, and most sumptuous articles of luxurious ornament, succeeded each other in rich and glittering profusion. Streams of people apparently without end poured on and on, jostling each other in the crowd and hurrying forward, scarcely seeming to notice the riches that surrounded them on every side; while vehicles of all shapes and makes, mingled up together in one moving mass like running water, lent their ceaseless roar to swell the noise and tumult.

As they dashed by the quickly-changing and ever-varying objects, it was curious to observe in what a strange procession they passed before the eye. Emporiums of splendid dresses, the materials brought from every quarter of the world; tempting stores of everything to stimulate and pamper the sated appetite and give new relish to the oft-repeated feast; vessels of burnished gold and silver, wrought into every exquisite form of vase, and dish, and goblet; guns, swords, pistols, and patent engines of destruction; screws and irons for the crooked, clothes for the newly-born, drugs for the sick, coffins for the dead, churchyards for the buried – all these jumbled each with the other and flocking side by side, seemed to flit by in motley dance like the fantastic groups of the old Dutch painter, and with the same stern moral for the unheeding restless crowd.

Nor were there wanting objects in the crowd itself to give new point and purpose to the shifting scene. The rags of the squalid ballad-singer fluttered in the rich light that showed the goldsmith's treasures; pale and pinched-up faces hovered about the windows where there was tempting food; hungry eyes wandered over the profusion guarded by one thin sheet of brittle glass – an iron wall to them; half-naked shivering figures stopped to gaze at Chinese shawls and golden stuffs of India. There was a christening party at the largest coffin-maker's, and a funeral hatchment had stopped some great improvements in the bravest mansion. Life and death went hand in hand; wealth and poverty stood side by side; repletion and starvation laid them down together. (NN, ch. 32)

When Bagehot called Dickens a reporter of London life he was indicating his mastery of realistic detail. Trollope can write in similar fashion, as when he tells us in Chapter 14 of *The Belton Estate* (1865) that William Belton walks 'across St James's Square, across Jermyn Street, across Piccadilly, and up Bond Street', goes beyond Oxford

Street and wanders 'away into the far distance of Portman Square and Baker Street'. Thackeray is as familiar as Dickens with the topography of the capital, typically using settings from the world of high society and the professions: Mayfair, Bloomsbury, The Temple and clubland. But he is not so prolific with actual addresses. Where, for example, is Great Gaunt Street, where Pitt Crawley lives in *Vanity Fair*?

Dickens made his reputation as a young writer with his unprecedented accounts of life in the London streets in *Sketches by Boz*. In his subsequent writings, he pinpoints routes and addresses. When Bill Sikes and Oliver Twist are on their way out of London to Chertsey, where the burglary is to take place, they walk into Bethnal Green Road, and thread the streets between Shoreditch and Smithfield: 'Turning down Sun Street and Crown Street, and crossing Finsbury Square, Mr Sikes struck, by way of Chiswell Street, into Barbican: thence into Long Lane: and so into Smithfield.' When clear of Smithfield, they make their way through Hosier Lane into Holborn, pass Hyde Park, approach Kensington and then get a lift on a cart through Hammersmith, Chiswick, Kew Bridge and Brentford (OT, ch. 21). In *Little Dorrit*, Clennam, after crossing Smithfield with Pancks, is left alone 'at the corner of Barbican'. He turns down Aldersgate Street, goes towards Saint Paul's and finds the injured Cavaletto lying in a litter after being knocked down by a mail coach. These coaches, a bystander says, 'come a racing out of Lad Lane and Wood Street at twelve or fourteen mile an hour'. Clennam accompanies the litter to Saint Bartholomew's Hospital and makes his way home to Covent Garden via Snow Hill and Holborn (LD, I, ch. 13). A reader with a street map to hand can follow the progress of many a character through the 'great, confused city' (BH, ch. 19), as Dickens called it.

The streets and buildings that Dickens named so precisely immediately indicated to contemporary readers the social status or occupation of the people who lived there. Mrs Gamp lodges in Kingsgate Street, High Holborn, 'at a bird-fancier's next door but one to the celebrated mutton-pie shop, and directly opposite to the original cat's-meat warehouse; the renown of which establishments was duly heralded on their respective fronts' (MC, ch. 19). Further up the social scale, Mrs Wititterly lives in Cadogan Place, 'the connecting link between the aristocratic pavements of Belgrave Square, and the barbarism of Chelsea [a village in those days]. It is in Sloane Street, but not of it. The people in Cadogan Place look down upon Sloane Street, and think Brompton low. They affect fashion too, and wonder where the New Road is' (NN, ch. 21). Dickens goes back sixty years to the Gordon Riots of 1780 in *Barnaby Rudge*, but his sure and accurate detail (based on historical records as well as his own knowledge of the London streets) authenticates the rioters' destructive course through the city and the measures taken in defence.

London, with its various auras and connotations, seems more than a material presence in the novels though that reality was a firm basis for Dickens's messages of social reform. Its labyrinthine streets could frighten, as we have seen, and so they can possibly be regarded as emblematic of the fears and confusions besetting the lonely and helpless. Nothing shows Oliver Twist's vulnerability more clearly than the streets, ways and yards the Artful Dodger leads him through en route to Fagin's den or the wrong turning he takes on his errand for Mr Brownlow – a mistake that leads to his recapture. Tom-all-Alone's, the 'black, dilapidated street' where Jo tries to exist as a crossing-sweeper, breeds 'a crowd of foul existence' that is irredeemable (BH, ch. 16), a physical 'objective correlative' of the plight of wretchedly poor in early Victorian London. Disease and fog, in the same novel, are the most commonly cited of all of Dickens's so-called 'symbols'. The description of fog along with the dirt in the streets right at the beginning of the novel points at the outset to the concern in *Bleak House* with the bewildering machinations involved in the case of Jarndyce v. Jarndyce. The Lord Chancellor sits at the heart of the fog: 'Never can there come fog too thick, never can there come mud and mire too deep, to assort with the groping and floundering condition which this High Court of Chancery, most pestilent of hoary sinners, holds, this day, in the sight of heaven and earth' (BH, ch. 1). And we're prepared for ghosts and Scrooge's unseeing inhumanity in *A Christmas Carol* when we read of the dense fog making the houses opposite Scrooge's office 'mere phantoms' and see 'the dingy cloud come drooping down, obscuring everything' (ACC, Stave 1). Dickens told Forster that when he came to London as a boy he would go to the top of Bayham Street 'and look from it over the dust-heaps and dock-leaves and fields ... at the cupola of St Paul's looming through the smoke' (Forster, I, 1). Those dust-heaps, huge mounds of refuse and excrement, appear in *Our Mutual Friend* as sources of wealth. John Harmon's father had made his fortune in buying and selling them and in them could be found valuables and documents (such as the will discovered by Silas Wegg). The symbolism is obvious: wealth can be a dirty business.

But happiness can thrive in these unpromising urban settings. One of the *Sketches by Boz* is called 'London Recreations' and (as we have seen) he writes about Greenwich Fair, Astley's equestrian shows and theatres as well as grimmer places like pawnshops and Newgate Prison. Personal joys exist as well. In *Dombey and Son*, Florence and Walter walk together to a London church ('a mouldy old church in a yard') on their bridal morning, past luxurious shops, great houses and then darker and narrower streets. 'Lovingly and trustfully, through all the narrow yards and alleys and the shady streets, Florence goes, clinging to his arm, to be his wife' (DS, ch. 57).

Chapter Five
Social Class in Victorian England

The class system in Victorian England had three broad divisions: upper, middle and lower. In the first category were the aristocracy and the landed gentry. The second group were subdivided: the upper middle class included professional and business men along with well-to-do Church of England clergy; the lower middle class included clerks and small shop owners. Some people who belonged this last-named subdivision, on the border between the middle and lower classes, were given the epithet 'shabby-genteel'. The lower classes were the manual workers and their families, below whom were the unclassifiable thousands of poor and destitute men, women and children. People were expected to know their place. Mrs Cecil Alexander's hymn, 'All things bright and beautiful' (1848), frequently sung in churches, included the complacent verse (usually omitted nowadays): 'The rich man in his castle, The poor man at his gate, God made them, high or lowly, And order'd their estate.'

Limited movement across the class divisions was infrequent but possible in Victorian England. Successful industrialists, for instance, sometimes aspired to join the higher echelons of society – hence snobbery and gentlemanliness became topics of discussion as the novels of Thackeray and Trollope show. Dickens himself was an example of social mobility, having rapidly moved upwards thanks to his energy and literary achievement, but he knew that for most people a change of class was virtually impossible. In a speech he made to the Liverpool Mechanics' Institution on 26 February 1844, he favoured 'mutual forbearance among various classes' but declared that 'differences of wealth, of rank, of intellect' were inevitable. He thought that there was no fear of general dissatisfaction with one's station in life since the 'distinction of the different grades of society are so accurately marked, and so very difficult to pass'

(Fielding, 1988, pp. 56–57). Despite his contempt for the 'dandy insolence' (Letters, VII, p. 664) of Lord Palmerston and other upper-class leaders typically displayed at the time of the Crimean War (1853–56), he told the Administrative Reform Association in a speech on 27 June 1855 that he wished 'to avoid placing in opposition ... the two words Aristocracy and the People': 'I am one of those who can believe in the virtues and uses of both, and, I would elevate or depress neither, at the cost of a single just right belonging to the other' (Fielding, 1988, p. 203).

Dickens fills his fiction with people from all classes although the lower and middle classes predominate. He is concerned mostly with urban people – farmers and country people rarely appear in his work (though Mr Browdie in *Nicholas Nickleby* is one exception). Despite his declared belief, just quoted, that the aristocracy had its virtues and uses, he usually negatively depicts its representatives. Sir Mulberry Hawk and Lord Frederick Verisopht in *Nicholas Nickleby* are caricatures, as their names suggest. In *Bleak House*, the appropriately named Sir Leicester Dedlock, a baronet, who is opposed to ideas of democracy, is confronted by Mr Rouncewell, a self-made ironmaster from the north whose mother is ironically the housekeeper at Chesney Wold, Sir Leicester's country house. Mr Rouncewell, expressing himself with tact and dignity, thinks that Rosa, Lady Dedlock's maid, would make an unsuitable wife for his son Watt (whose name suggests affinities with James Watt and even Wat Tyler) because of her dependent and ill-educated status as a servant of the aristocratic classes. He does not regard 'the village school as teaching everything desirable to be known by [his] son's wife'. Sir Leicester is fearful of the social consequences implicit in the ironmaster's attitude.

> From the village school of Chesney Wold, intact as it is this minute, to the whole framework of society: from the whole framework of society, to the aforesaid framework receiving tremendous cracks in consequence of people (ironmasters, lead-mistresses, and what not) not minding their catechism, and getting out of the station unto which they are called – necessarily and for ever, according to Sir Leicester's rapid logic, the first station in which they happen to find themselves; and from that, to their educating other people out of *their* stations,

and so obliterating the landmarks, and opening the floodgates, and all the rest of it; this is the swift progress of the Dedlock mind.

But Sir Leicester answers courteously and 'with all the nature of gentleman shining in him' offers Mr Rouncewell hospitality for the night (BH, ch. 28).

Another principled man of the industrialized middle classes is Daniel Doyce in *Little Dorrit*, an engineer and inventor, who is angered and frustrated by the upper-class inefficiency and indifference of the Circumlocution Office and takes his skills abroad to 'a certain barbaric Power' (LD, II, ch. 22), which honours him for his achievements. Other men from the upper stratum of the middle class in Dickens's fiction use their money and influence benevolently, such as Mr Brownlow (in *Oliver Twist*), the Cheeryble Brothers (in *Nicholas Nickleby*) and Mr Jarndyce (in *Bleak House*), though some critics find their actions unbelievable. But Dickens also portrays among middle-class businessmen the selfishness of Scrooge (in *A Christmas Carol*), the heartless ruthlessness of Ralph Nickleby, the cold pride of Mr Dombey, the hypocritical boastfulness of Bounderby (in *Hard Times*), who has made his money in Coketown, and the shallow pretensions of the Veneerings (in *Our Mutual Friend*).

Moving down the social scale but staying among professional people, we find portraits of good and bad lawyers, doctors, clergymen and schoolteachers and especially fond depictions of shabby-genteel people like Dick Swiveller (in *The Old Curiosity Shop*), the Cratchits (in *A Christmas Carol*), the Micawbers (in *David Copperfield*) and the Wilfers (in *Our Mutual Friend*). Dickens always has profound sympathies for the poor lower classes, including paupers and deprived and neglected children right at the bottom of society, usually endowing them with virtuous qualities: Jo (in *Bleak House*), the Plornishes, Nandy and Maggie (in *Little Dorrit*) and Betty Higden (in *Our Mutual Friend*). The class demarcation is usually inflexible, as he himself sometimes implied, although Dickens appeals directly – or more often indirectly – to his readers for an understanding of – and sympathy with-- the underprivileged. His apostrophe on the death of Jo, the crossing-sweeper, in *Bleak House* is a striking outburst: 'Dead, your Majesty. Dead, my lords and gentlemen, Dead, Right Reverends and Wrong Reverends of every order. Dead, men and women, born with Heavenly compassion in your hearts. And dying thus around us every day' (BH, ch. 47).

He emphasizes the importance of integrity, hard work and effort, whatever the social class of the people concerned. David Copperfield, who is partly modelled on himself but who comes from a slightly higher stratum of the class into which Dickens was born, strives for success in love and authorship, urged on by his great-aunt, Miss Trotwood. She tells him that she wants him to be 'a firm fellow. A fine firm fellow, with a will of your own. With resolution ... With determination. With character, Trot. With strength of character that is not to be influenced, except on good reason, by anybody, or by anything' (DC, ch. 19). David is later set on helping his aunt out of her financial difficulties and on marrying Dora: 'What I had to do, was, to turn the painful discipline of my younger days to account, by going to work with a resolute and steady heart. What I had to do, was, to take my woodman's axe in my hand, and clear my own way through the forest of difficulty, by cutting down the trees, until I came to Dora' (DC, ch. 36). But Pip, in *Great Expectations*, idles his time away in London when he is given money by an unknown benefactor in order to become a gentleman and is cured of his selfishness only by humiliation when he discovers that the source of his wealth is Magwitch, a former criminal. The true gentleman in that novel turns out to be Joe Gargery, the village blacksmith, who had been Pip's surrogate father. Another reformation is that of Eugene Wrayburn in *Our Mutual Friend*, who – unlike Pip – was born into a privileged world. He is an idle and world-weary young barrister from the upper classes of a type Dickens had previously portrayed in the person of James Harthouse in *Hard Times*. Later readers of the novel compared Wrayburn to an Oscar Wilde character. He falls in love with Lizzie Hexam, the daughter of a Thames boatman. She reciprocates his love, although unable to admit her feelings because of the social disparity. Bradley Headstone, the schoolmaster, who also loves Lizzie and has struggled to attain middle-class respectability, bitterly resents Eugene's apparently effortless superiority. Nevertheless, Eugene reforms and he and Lizzie eventually marry, shocking the moneyed and aristocratic circle in which he moved. Twemlow, one of that circle, speaks up for the young couple in some of the last words of the novel: 'if such feelings induced this gentleman to marry this lady, I think he is the greater gentleman for the action, and makes her the greater lady' (OMF, IV, Chapter the Last). That is the most remarkable example in Dickens's novels of the breaking of class barriers.

Chapter Six
Nicholas Nickleby, The Old Curiosity Shop, Barnaby Rudge

Nicholas Nickleby (1838–39)

The title of the original serialized version shows that this novel is a lengthy picaresque narrative like the *Pickwick Papers*: *The Life and Adventures of Nicholas Nickleby, Containing a Faithful Account of the Fortunes, Misfortunes, Uprisings, Downfallings and Complete Career of the Nickleby Family, edited by 'Boz'*. Following the death of Mr Nickleby senior, Nicholas Nickleby, his sister, Kate, and his mother seek help from Ralph Nickleby, the late Mr Nickleby's brother, a rich and ruthless businessman, but he shows them scant sympathy. Nicholas is compelled to find work as an assistant teacher at Dotheboys Hall in Yorkshire, a boys' boarding school run by the ignorant and cruel Wackford Squeers. He rescues the wretched Smike from the clutches of Squeers. The two of them return temporarily to London but then walk to Portsmouth, where they fall in with Vincent Crummles's travelling theatrical company. Meanwhile, Kate has had to become an assistant in Madame Mantalini's millinery establishment in London and is forced to resist the amorous advances of Sir Mulberry Hawk, an aristocratic roué. Nicholas's fortunes improve when he becomes an employee of the benevolent Cheeryble brothers but he has to frustrate a plot to marry off Madeline Bray, the young woman he loves, to the elderly Arthur Gride. The novel ends in the disclosure of secrets in typical melodramatic fashion with the revelation that Smike is Ralph Nickleby's son and with Ralph's suicide. These surprising discoveries are soon followed by the marriages of Nicholas with Madeline and of Kate with Frank Cheeryble.

The novel is especially rich in characters and events, as was shown in David Edgar's triumphant dramatization for the Royal Shakespeare Company in 1980. Two sequences in the novel are outstanding: Nicholas's experiences at Dotheboys Hall and with Crummles's company. Dickens exposed in the first of these the appalling scandal of those Yorkshire schools that in exchange for fees kept unwanted or illegitimate boys out of the way of their parents or guardians. In the second, Dickens revelled in the portrayal of actors and actresses on the road – the theatre in all its forms was something he adored. Despite its exposure of social wrongs, aristocratic immorality and sordid mercenary machinations, the novel is shot through with comedy, as in Mr Mantalini's conversation, Fanny Squeers's indignant letter to Ralph Nickleby about Nicholas's treatment of her father, the doings of the Crummles's company, the eccentric behaviour of Mrs Nickleby's neighbour (the 'gentleman in small clothes') and the typically Dickensian black humour of Squeers's educational system. Readers found – and still find – it difficult to accept the altruism of the Cheeryble brothers but Dickens based them on two wealthy Manchester merchants, David and William Grant. He wrote in the Preface to the first edition that 'their liberal charity, their singleness of heart, their noble nature, and their unbounded benevolence, are no creations of the Author's brain; but are prompting every day (and oftenest by stealth) some munificent and generous deed in that town of which they are the pride and honour.' Another character modelled on an actual person is Mrs Nickleby, whose wonderfully surrealistic streams of consciousness derive from his mother's conversation. Those who think that Nicholas Nickleby is a colourless central figure should bear in mind Dickens's assertion in his 1848 Preface to the first cheap edition that he is 'a young man of an impetuous temper and of little or no experience' and that Dickens therefore 'saw no reason why such a hero should be lifted out of nature.' It seems appropriate that Dickens dedicated the novel to his friend William Macready, the celebrated actor of the day.

The Old Curiosity Shop (1840–41)

The story began as an episode in Dickens's periodical, *Master Humphrey's Clock*, but he quickly expanded it into a full-length independent novel. The heroine, the thirteen-year-old Nell Trent (popularly known as Little Nell), lives with her grandfather in his curiosity shop in London. He is a secret gambler, whose losses put him in the power of the evil Daniel Quilp, who takes possession of the shop and who lusts after Nell. Nell and her grandfather (who is now physically and mentally enfeebled) make a stealthy escape and wander wherever chance and inclination take them. On their journeys they meet comic, benevolent and malevolent people, including Codlin and Short (travelling Punch and Judy men), Mrs Jarley (the proprietress of a waxwork show) and a kindly school-master. They find eventual refuge in a village where, exhausted and frail, Nell dies. Soon afterwards, her broken-hearted grandfather also dies, while seated on her grave. In contrast to the sweet and virtuous Nell is the demonic Quilp, who does his utmost to track the couple down. A key character is Dick Swiveller, who partly under the influence of the little servant girl he affectionately calls the Marchioness, reforms his drunken irresponsible ways and helps to expose Quilp's machinations. When Quilp realizes that his plot against Kit Nubbles, Nell's faithful young admirer, has been found out he tries to escape and is drowned in the Thames. The novel ends with other evil characters (like Sampson and Sally Brass) suitably punished and with the virtuous rewarded with future lives of happiness.

Dickens's portrayal of Nell, influenced by his memories of Mary Hogarth, is like that of Oliver Twist. In his Preface to the first cheap edition (1848), he observed that in writing the book he had it 'always in [his] fancy to surround the lonely figure of the child with grotesque and wild but not impossible companions, and to gather about her innocent face and pure intentions, associates as strange and uncongenial as the grim objects that are about her bed when her history is first foreshadowed [in Chapter 2].' With its polarities of extreme good and evil and with its blend of fairy tale and realism, the novel is variously found disturbing, sentimental and faulty in structure. Its characters, incidents and sayings have not passed into common usage as so many of Dickens's have, although Dick Swiveller has had admirers, including J.B. Priestley, who devoted an essay to him in his essays on *The English Comic Characters* (Priestley, 1925, pp. 224–40).

But it was hugely popular at the time, selling 100,000 copies a week in its serialized form and making an unprecedented emotional impact on its first readers. One example of those readers was Francis Jeffrey, who in his younger days was a cutting critic of Romantic poets but who declared that there had been 'nothing so good as Nell since Cordelia'. On the other hand, fifty years later Oscar Wilde famously said that 'One must have a heart of stone to read the death of Nell without laughing' (Ford, 1965, pp. 55–57). But as always in Dickens there are powerful passages of terror, pity and humour: Quilp at the breakfast table (eating, to begin with, 'hard eggs, shell and all'), the Marchioness's encounters with Dick Swiveller, and the Nubbles family ecstatic with enjoyment at Astley's equestrian show, to choose only three.

Barnaby Rudge (1841)

Barnaby Rudge: A Tale of the Riots of '80, which immediately followed *The Old Curiosity Shop* as a weekly serial in *Master Humphrey's Clock*, is one of Dickens's two historical novels – the other is *A Tale of Two Cities*. The eponymous main character is an innocent simpleton and the central figure in the two plots: a murder story and a basically factual account of the Gordon Riots that took place in London in June 1780. (The uprising was instigated by Lord George Gordon to protest against the removal of certain restrictions on Roman Catholics.) Barnaby is the son of a murderer who has been in hiding for over twenty years, who then haunts Mrs Rudge (his supposed widow) and others as a mysterious Stranger and who is finally brought to justice and hanged. Barnaby gets dangerously involved in the Gordon Riots without any awareness of the religious and political issues. He is sentenced to death but is reprieved. Dickens's vivid presentation of near revolutionary violence shows his abhorrence of mob rule combined with his fascination with crime and punishment. A menacing and disturbing figure who takes a delight in violence is Hugh, the ostler at the Maypole Inn. He is revealed to be the illegitimate son of Sir Edward Chester and is hanged for his part in the riots. Another form of conflict in the novel is tension in family relationships – Sir John and Edward Chester, John and Joe Willet, Gabriel Varden and his wife, Mrs Rudge and her husband.

Critics today concentrate on these predominant features and overlook two others that pleased contemporary readers. The first of these is the progress and difficulties of the course of young love. Joe Willett, the son of John Willett, the landlord of the Maypole Inn, is in love with the dainty and flirtatious Dolly Varden, who was made even more popular by her portrait painted by Frith (commissioned by Dickens with a portrait of Kate Nickleby as a companion piece) and by her depictions by Phiz. Their courtship is paralleled by that between Edward Chester, the son of the Protestant Sir Edward Chester, and Emma Haredale, the daughter of the Catholic Mr Haredale. The second entertaining element is the tart or black comedy in Dickens's presentation of Miggs (the Vardens' maid-of-all-work), the piously protestant Mrs Varden, Sim Tappertit (Gabriel's apprentice in his trade of locksmith), Ned Dennis the hangman and the languidly aristocratic Sir Edward Chester. Two contrasting characters have a central presence: Gabriel Varden, the worthy locksmith, and Grip, Barnaby Rudge's malicious pet raven. Dickens in his Preface to the novel emphasized its serious purpose, insisting that its message was that intolerance and persecution must be exposed and that the Gordon Riots were therefore a 'good lesson' to us all. Interest in this novel flagged for some time in the twentieth century but has revived with the publication of several new editions: in the Everyman Dickens (edited by Donald Hawes, 1996), World's Classics (edited by Clive Hurst, 2003), Penguin Classics (edited by John Bowen, 2003) and Everyman's Library (introduced by Peter Ackroyd, 2005).

Chapter Seven
Prisons and Crime

In his life and works Dickens was profoundly interested in questions of crime and punishment. As a boy he had become painfully acquainted with the Marshalsea Prison in the Southwark area of London when his father was gaoled for debt in 1824. As a very young man, before his writing career fully began, he worked for a time as a lawyer's clerk and then as a journalist whose assignments included reporting on law cases. He had a lifelong interest in questions of capital punishment and methods of imprisonment. As an established novelist and public figure, he visited prisons in England (such as Coldbath Fields and Newgate in London) and America in 1842 (where the Eastern Penitentary in Philadelphia disturbed him with its strict regime). He was present at three or four public executions of criminals, including the hangings of François Courvoisier at Newgate Prison on 6 July 1840 and of Mr and Mrs Manning at Horsemonger Lane Gaol on 13 November 1849 and the beheading of a criminal in Rome in 1845. Thackeray was also present at Courvoisier's execution and wrote an unforgettable account, 'Going to See a Man Hanged', published in August 1840 in *Fraser's Magazine*. Such spectacles filled Dickens (like Thackeray) with revulsion, and for many years he advocated the abolition of capital punishment, though in later years he thought it a necessity. His frighteningly macabre Ned Dennis, the hangman in *Barnaby Rudge*, was modelled on the actual hangman of the same name, who unlike his fictional counterpart was reprieved from execution when the Gordon Riots were over. Maria Manning was probably the model for Dickens's Mademoiselle Hortense, who murders Mr Tulkinghorn in *Bleak House*.

Dickens accompanied policemen on their tours of inspection in London, and was on friendly terms with some of them, notably Inspector Charles Frederick Field of the small Metropolitan Detective

Force that had been formed in 1842. His *Reprinted Pieces* originally published in *All the Year Round*, include 'On Duty with Inspector Field', 'The Detective Police' (featuring an Inspector Wield) and 'Three "Detective" Anecdotes' (also with Wield). 'Down with the Tide', another of the *Reprinted Pieces*, is an account of a journey on the Thames in the Thames Police Galley.

Crime, mystery and detection were favourite subjects in the fiction written by Dickens's contemporaries. When he started writing, so-called Newgate novels (named after the London prison) were popular, written by Bulwer-Lytton, Harrison Ainsworth and others, who were inclined to glamorize criminals and highwaymen, as in Bulwer-Lytton's *Eugene Aram* (1832) and Ainsworth's *Rookwood* (1834), which has Dick Turpin as its hero. In the middle of the nineteenth century, sensation novels, like *Lady Audley's Secret* (1862) by Mary Elizabeth Braddon, were all the rage, with their plots of secrets and nefarious doings. Wilkie Collins, one of Dickens's closest friends in his latter years, wrote (among much else) his best-selling novels, *The Woman in White* (1860) and *The Moonstone* (1868), constructed as ingenious stories of crime and mystery. Both novels were first serialized in Dickens's magazine, *All the Year Round*, and may have stimulated him to write *The Mystery of Edwin Drood* at the end of his career.

Criminal activity in the London underworld is one of the most striking features of his second novel, *Oliver Twist*, with its spirited thieves' jargon , its closely observed picture of Fagin's den and its horrific presentation of Bill Sikes's murderous attack on Nancy. As we have seen, Dickens asserted that in that novel his depictions of crime were realistic, but it is possible to see also his compassion for the wretchedness of some of the people (particularly children and the poor) caught up in a criminal environment. In the early part of the novel Dickens describes the intolerably dirty cell in which little Oliver is temporarily locked up: 'in our station-houses, men and women are every night confined on the most trivial *charges* – the word is worth noting – in dungeons, compared with which, those in Newgate – occupied by the most atrocious felons, tried, found guilty, and under sentence of death – are palaces' (OT, ch. 11). Dickens sympathetically considers Nancy's tortured feelings in the same novel: her 'life had been squandered in the streets, and among the most noisome of the stews and dens of London, but there was something of the woman's original nature left in her still' – but he goes on to say that she thought it a weakness to betray any gleam of womanly feeling (OT, ch. 40).

Turning from the subject of the criminal urban underworld, we note that in Dickens's novels murders take place in *Martin Chuzzlewit* (Jonas clubs Montague Tigg to death), *Bleak House* (Mlle Hortense shoots Tulkinghorn), *A Tale of Two Cities* (Gaspard stabs the Marquis to death), *Our Mutual Friend* (George Radford is murdered in a riverside lodging-house) and almost certainly in *The Mystery of Edwin Drood* (since it is likely that Jasper killed Drood). Twenty-two years before the action of *Barnaby Rudge* begins, Mr Rudge has killed Reuben Haredale and the gardener. In *Great Expectations*, Orlick's brutal assault on Mrs Gargery with a convict's leg-iron eventually leads to her death.

With the exception of Nancy's murder, Dickens does not usually dwell on the details of the crime but expresses his fascination with the workings of the mind and conscience of the murderer after the deed has been committed. Bill Sikes, making his way north of London to escape from the room where he had killed Nancy, cannot rid himself of the sight of her corpse, a vision that seems to be pursuing him: 'Every object before him, substance or shadow, still or moving, took the semblance of some fearful thing; but these fears were nothing compared to the sense that haunted him of that morning's ghastly figure following at his heels' (OT, ch. 48).

Jonas Chuzzlewit feels no sorrow for murdering Tigg but is immediately afterwards overwhelmed by 'dread and fear' and recalls the bedroom where he had spent the previous two nights thinking of what he was determined to do:

This made him, in a gloomy, murderous, mad way, not only fearful *for* himself, but *of* himself; for being, as it were, a part of the room: a something supposed to be there, yet missing from it: he invested himself with its mysterious terrors; and when he pictured in his mind the ugly chamber, false and quiet, false and quiet, through the dark hours of two nights; and the tumbled bed, and he not in it, though believed to be; he became in a manner his own ghost and phantom, and was at once the haunting spirit and the haunted man. (MC, ch. 47)

Perhaps Dickens would have developed even more subtly the tormented feelings of John Jasper at the end of *The Mystery of Edwin Drood*? Guilt, repentance and consequences of evil fascinated him.

Financial swindles, often in the news in mid-Victorian England, are prominent in his fiction. Montague Tigg (in *Martin Chuzzlewit*) sets up the fraudulent Anglo-Bengalee Disinterested Loan and Life Assurance Company, and Uriah Heep is sentenced to transportation for 'fraud, forgery, and conspiracy' (DC, ch. 61). Mr Merdle, the powerful and respected financier and banker, commits suicide by cutting his jugular vein with a penknife. He is then discovered to have been 'simply the greatest Forger and the greatest Thief that ever cheated the gallows' (LD, II, ch. 25). Dickens based Merdle on two contemporary business men: George Hudson (1800–71), the so-called 'Railway King', and John Sadlier (1814–56), a banker who poisoned himself on Hampstead Heath. At the back of Dickens's mind were probably his father's money problems and his own determination to make himself financially secure.

Dickens's friendship with Inspector Field contributed to his portrait of Inspector Bucket, the first professional detective in English fiction, who conducts a number of investigations in *Bleak House*, pursuing Gridley, identifying Mlle Hortense as the murderer of Mr Tulkinghorn, tracing Lady Dedlock's route to her death at the gates of the graveyard where her lover was buried and compelling Smallweed to hand over a vital bill. Dickens makes Bucket as keenly observant as he was in his progress through the London streets. His questions are sharp but he is imperturbable and deceptively pleasant. His wife is 'a lady of a natural detective genius' (BH, ch. 63), whose watchful eyes are of invaluable help to him. The scene when he exposes and arrests Hortense comes to a climax with her declaring that she would love to tear Mrs Bucket from limb to limb: ' "Bless you, darling," says Mr Bucket, with the greatest composure; "I'm fully prepared to hear that"' (BH, ch. 54).

Dickens had earlier introduced an investigator into his fiction in the person of Nadgett, an enquiry agent in *Martin Chuzzlewit*. Higher up the scale of legal officialdom are magistrates, judges and lawyers, who are viewed in the novels with hostility or satire – the frightening Mr Fang in *Oliver Twist* and Mr Justice Stareleigh and the absurdly bombastic Serjeant Buzfuz in the *Pickwick Papers* are three of the most memorable representatives of judicial authority, based on officials he had seen in action when he was a young reporter in the 1830s.

Many commentators have noted the presence in his fiction of prisons, perhaps because he never forgot his father's plight or, more significantly, his own anguish at the time. *Sketches by Boz* includes a grim account of 'A Visit to Newgate' and there are prison scenes in many of his novels from *Pickwick Papers* onwards. Mr Pickwick, sent to the Fleet Prison because he refuses to pay the £750 fine in the Bardell v. Pickwick case, is appalled and fascinated by seeing the many classes of people who have been locked up: 'from the labouring-man in his fustian jacket, to the broken-down spendthrift in his shawl dressing-gown, most appropriately out at elbows; but there was the same air about them all – a listless jail-bird careless swagger, a vagabondish who's-afraid sort of bearing, which is wholly indescribable in words, but which any man can understand in one moment if he wish, by setting foot in the nearest debtor's prison, and looking at the very first group of people he sees there' (PP, ch. 41). Dickens's fullest presentation of punishment for debt is in *Little Dorrit*, where with pity, satire and grim humour he presents a picture of life in the Marshalsea, 'a close and confined prison for debtors' that contained within it 'a much closer and more confined jail for smugglers (LD, I, ch. 6). There Mr Dorrit and his family were imprisoned long before the action of the novel begins – his youngest child, Amy (Little Dorrit), was born there.

Much more terrifying is Newgate, where Fagin is confined in the condemned cell 'like sitting in a vault strewn with dead bodies' (OT, ch. 52). Barnaby Rudge and others are sent there to await execution or reprieve after their participation in the Gordon Riots. In *A Tale of Two Cities*, long imprisonment in the Bastille has temporarily deprived Doctor Manette of his wits and later in the novel in 'the black prison of the Conciergerie, the doomed of the day [among them, Charles Darnay] await their fate' (ATTC, III, ch. 13) during the Reign of Terror in the French Revolution.

Dickens was always interested in penal practice and reform and glances satirically at one of its manifestations in *David Copperfield*. Mr Creakle, David's former schoolmaster, has become a Middlesex Magistrate responsible for a prison run on the so-called Silent

System, in which the prisoners remained in complete isolation, leading (Dickens sarcastically remarks) to 'sincere contrition and repentance' (DC, ch. 61). Two of its model prisoners are Littimer (formerly Steerforth's manservant) and Uriah Heep (the scheming clerk who had worked for Mr Wickfield).

As with the fog in *Bleak House*, the presence of prisons in Dickens's fiction has been interpreted as symbolic, notably in *Little Dorrit*, where characters of all kinds (Mrs Clennam, Mr Merdle, Miss Wade, for example) can be seen as confined or inhibited by circumstances and their own personalities.

Chapter Eight
Dickens and Education

In Dickens's lifetime, no nationwide system of children's education existed in England. At the beginning of the nineteenth century, the British and Foreign Society and the Church of England Society made the education of the poor one of their principal concerns. From 1833, the Government gave some financial support to these Societies, eventually establishing a School Inspectorate and teachers' training colleges. Private schools of all kinds existed, ranging from the 'ragged schools' for the destitute (which Dickens supported and visited) and charity schools to the old-established grammar schools for boys. The privileged classes sent their sons to the great public schools, such as Eton, Harrow, Winchester and Rugby, and employed governesses to teach their daughters. Girls of the poorer classes had little or no education. It was not until 1870, the year of Dickens's death, that after years of controversy the foundations for universal compulsory schooling were laid with W.E. Forster's Education Act, part of the legislation of Gladstone's reforming Liberal Government.

Dickens himself had little conventional schooling. In his boyhood days in Chatham, he and his sister Fanny attended a dame school and he then went to a school run by the Reverend William Giles, of whom he always had fond memories. When the *Pickwick Papers* was coming out, Giles sent him a silver snuff box with an inscription, 'The Inimitable Boz'. After Dickens arrived in London at the age of ten, he was not sent to school at first. But on leaving Warren's Blacking Warehouse, he was sent to the Wellington House Academy in the Hampstead Road for two years, probably between 1825 and 1827. The headmaster was Mr William Jones, who is thought to be the original of the fearsome Mr Creakle, who runs Salem House school in *David Copperfield*. In 'Our School' (one of his *Reprinted Pieces*), Dickens wrote that 'the only branches of education with which [the master] showed the least acquaintance' were ruling ciphering-books 'with a bloated mahogany ruler, or smiting the palms of offenders with the same diabolical instrument, or viciously drawing a pair of pantaloons tight with one of his large hands, and caning the wearer with the other'.

It is conventionally said that Dickens's education lay mainly in his observation of the life around him, particularly in the London streets, but this is to overlook his enthusiastic reading of a range of books even when he was very young. Identifying himself with the fictional hero, he recalls some of his literary favourites in *David Copperfield*: seventeenth and eighteenth-century fiction (*Roderick Random, Peregrine Pickle, Humphry Clinker, Tom Jones, The Vicar of Wakefield, Don Quixote, Gil Blas* and *Robinson Crusoe*) as well as the *Arabian Nights* (which was always important to him) and the *Tales of the Genii*. Shakespeare and the Bible, as Grahame Smith has pointed out, were 'formative at the level of language, structure, character and theme' in his writing (Smith, 1996, p. 41). As for the education of his own children, the boys were sent to school at various establishments in England and abroad. His eldest son, Charles, was at Eton for two years (his fees paid by Miss Angela Burdett-Coutts) but Henry was the only one who went to a university – Cambridge, where he was a student at Trinity Hall. As was customary among the middle and upper classes, Dickens's two daughters, Mamie and Kate, were educated at home by governesses.

Dickens describes about thirty schools in his writings – the fullest and best-known of his depictions are Dotheboys Hall in *Nicholas Nickleby*, Dr Blimber's school in *Dombey and Son*, Mr Creakle's school in *David Copperfield* and Mr M'Choakumchild's school in *Hard Times*. More specialized establishments, which he treats with a comic touch, include dancing academies run by Signor Billsmethi (in 'The Dancing Academy' in *Sketches by Boz*) and Mr Turveydrop (in *Bleak House*) and Mr Pecksniff's school for architects (in *Martin Chuzzlewit*). Dickens portrays at least twenty other teachers : elementary schoolmasters (Charley Hexam and Bradley Headstone (in *Our Mutual Friend*), private tutors like Mr Matthew Pocket (in *Great Expectations*), governesses like Ruth Pinch (in *Martin Chuzzlewit*) , 'Our Schoolmaster' (in *Sketches by Boz*) and many more. Unlike Thackeray (who went to Charterhouse and Trinity

College, Cambridge) and Trollope (who went to Harrow), Dickens does not fully enter the world of the public schools and universities, although Mr Feeder (a master at Dr Blimber's school) has a BA (a degree that Dickens satirically repeats a number of times); Dr Strong's school in *David Copperfield* was possibly suggested by the King's School, Canterbury; Sydney Carton (in *A Tale of Two Cities*) was at Shrewsbury School; Mr Matthew Pocket (in *Great Expectations*) was educated at Harrow and Cambridge; and Steerforth (in *David Copperfield*) went to Oxford.

Dickens's aim at the beginning of *Nicholas Nickleby* was to expose what he called the 'cheap Yorkshire schools', which in exchange for fees took unwanted or illegitimate boys (usually from the south of England), purporting to educate them but in fact cruelly treating them – half-starving them, making them do menial tasks and not allowing them holidays. In his Preface to the cheap edition (1848), Dickens described the Yorkshire schoolmasters as 'ignorant, sordid, brutal men, to whom few considerate persons would have entrusted the board and lodging of a horse or a dog'. Before writing the novel, he and Hablot K. Browne ('Phiz'), his illustrator, made a winter journey to Yorkshire to investigate the schools for themselves. Dotheboys Hall was based on Bowes Academy, near Greta Bridge, run by William Shaw. Dickens's chapters on Dotheboys Hall – in which he describes the wretched condition of the boys, Wackford Squeers's 'practical mode of teaching' (NN, ch. 8), Mrs Squeers's administration of brimstone and treacle, the pathetic figure of Smike, and Nicholas's flogging of Squeers – are unforgettable in their evocation of the harsh regime. At the same time, Dickens writes with such comic wit and verve that we relish details like the letter Fanny Squeers sends to Ralph Nickleby protesting at Nicholas's punishment of her father: 'My pa requests me to write to you, the doctors considering it doubtful whether he will ever recuvver the use of his legs which prevents his holding a pen' (NN, ch. 15). Does humour like this – and such names as 'Wackford' and 'Dotheboys' – detract from Dickens's message? Evidently not – his memorable presentation of people and scenes led to the closure of some of the schools and to an amelioration of the conditions it described.

Besides the particular abuses that Dickens highlighted in *Nicholas Nickleby*, there were general educational attitudes and practices that he felt were in need of remedy. He objected to what he considered to be the force-feeding of children's minds with inessential facts. The stimulation of their imaginations, such as he had experienced in his childhood reading of Fielding, Smollett and the *Arabian Nights,* was essential. In *Dombey and Son*, the six-year-old Paul is enthralled by the stories that Old Glubb tells him as he wheels him along the beach at Brighton in a little carriage: 'he knows all about the deep sea, and the fish that are in it, and the great monsters that come and lie on rocks in the sun, and dive into the water again when they're startled, blowing and splashing so, that they can be heard for miles' (DS, ch. 12). On the other hand, the 'young gentlemen' at Doctor Blimber's school, to which Paul has been sent, 'knew no rest from the pursuit of stony-hearted verbs, savage noun-substantives, inflexible syntactic passages, and ghosts of exercises that appeared to them in their dreams' (DS, ch. 11). The assistant master, the appropriately named Mr Feeder, BA, on one occasion 'had his Virgil stop on, and was slowly grinding that tune to four young gentleman' (DS, ch. 12).

In the same novel, Mr Dombey states that he is 'far from being friendly … to what is called by persons of levelling sentiments, general education' but that he thinks it necessary 'that the inferior classes should continue to be taught to know their position, and to conduct themselves properly' (DS, ch. 5). He therefore insists that Rob, the Toodles's son, should attend a charity school, run by the Charitable Grinders. The result is that Rob is 'huffed and cuffed, and flogged and badged, and taught, as parrots are, by a brute jobbed into the place of schoolmaster with as much fitness for it as a hound' (DS, ch. 20), and inevitably goes to the bad when he leaves the school. Uriah Heep and his father were brought up 'at a foundation school for boys' and his mother 'at a public, sort of charitable establishment'. He tells David Copperfield that they were taught to be 'umble to this person, and umble to that; and to pull off our caps here, and to make bows there; and always to know our place, and abase ourselves before our betters' (DC, ch. 39).

Even more rigid and restrictive is Mr Gradgrind's school, with Mr M'Choakumchild as its headmaster, in Dickens's attack on utilitarianism in *Hard Times*. One of the gentlemen witnessing the conduct of a lesson at the beginning of the book lays down the law to the schoolchildren: 'You are to be in all things regulated and governed ... by fact. We hope to have, before long, a board of fact, composed of commissioners of fact, who will force the people to be a people of fact, and of nothing but fact. You must discard the word Fancy altogether' (HT, I, ch. 2). Dickens tells us that 'no little Gradgrind had ever learnt the silly jingle, Twinkle, twinkle, little star; how I wonder what you are! No little Gradgrind had ever known wonder on the subject, each little Gradgrind having at five years old dissected the Great Bear like a Professor Owen [the prominent scientist of the day], and driven Charles's Wain like a locomotive engine-driver' (HT, I, ch. 3). He opposes this outlook on learning and life with the need for entertainment, obtainable at Mr Sleary's horse-riding circus, which is visiting Coketown. The lisping Sleary declares to an indignant Mr Gradgrind that 'People must be amuthed, Thquire, somehow' (HT, I. ch. 7). Warm-hearted Sissy Jupe, whose father was one of Sleary's riders, is placed in sharp and meaningful contrast to the bloodless Bitzer, a model pupil at the Coketown school. In *Our Mutual Friend*, Bradley Headstone, who is a trained teacher and who takes Charley Hexam under his wing as a pupil-teacher, is another schoolmaster who sets a value on factual learning; 'he had acquired mechanically a great store of teacher's knowledge' and 'from his early childhood up, his mind had been a place of mechanical stowage' (OMF, II, ch. 1).

But at least the school where Headstone teaches is better than the school Charley Hexam attended as a boy. In his picture of the latter institution, Dickens is apparently describing a ragged school, with its worthy aim of educating poor girls and boys. Its chaotic administration is completely opposite to the rigid regime imposed by Mr M'Choakumchild and typified by a schoolmaster like Headstone. But its 'atmosphere was oppressive and disagreeable; it was crowded, noisy and confusing ... The teachers, animated solely by good intentions, had no idea of execution, and a lamentable jumble was the upshot of their kind endeavours' (OMF, II, ch. 1).

One model of good education is Doctor Strong's school in Canterbury (in *David Copperfield*), where David is sent at the age of twelve or thirteen by his great-aunt, Miss Betsey Trotwood, although Dickens is vague about its curriculum and organization. It 'was an excellent school; as different from Mr Creakle's as good is from evil. It was very gravely and decorously ordered, and on a sound system; with an appeal, in everything, to the honour and good faith of the boys, and an avowed intention to rely on their possession of those qualities unless they proved themselves unworthy of it, which worked wonders.' The sixty-two year-old Doctor, who is constantly engaged on 'looking out for Greek roots' in his never-ending preparation of a new Dictionary, is 'the idol of the whole school' (DC, ch. 16). David becomes 'great in Latin verses' and is praised by Doctor Strong as a promising young scholar (DC, ch. 18). Another kindly schoolmaster, in a humbler station, is Mr Marton, in *The Old Curiosity Shop*, who is 'the very image of meekness and simplicity' as he sits among the din of the village classroom (OCS, ch. 25).

Dickens writes comparatively little about girls' schools, which were given scant attention anyway in the English society of his time. He mostly treats them and their teachers in a light-hearted or mocking manner. Three women teachers are Miss Monflathers, the headmistress of a Boarding and Day establishment for girls, who rebukes Little Nell for her unfemininity in helping to look after Mrs Jarley's waxworks (in *The Old Curiosity Shop*); Miss Peecher, 'small, shining, neat, methodical, and buxom', who teaches in the girls' division of the school where Bradley Headstone and Charley Hexam work and who is a secret admirer of Headstone (OMF, II, ch. 1); and Miss Twinkleton, the principal of the Seminary for Young Ladies in Cloisterham, notable for her two personalities, one as a schoolmistress and the other as a sprightly gossip (in *The Mystery of Edwin Drood*).

Dickens held to no clearly stated or formal educational theory or policy just as he held to no clearly defined principles of politics and religion. He believed that everyone, including working-class adults, was entitled to an appropriate form of education. We know from his novels, as we have just seen, that he thought that the teaching of children should be informed with qualities of imagination and sympathy and that coercion and cramming should be avoided – an obvious principle, perhaps, but one that needed to be impressed on those responsible for education in those days when it had first become an essential issue in British society. It was an issue, too, that was inseparable from questions of religion. Dickens's approach was informed by a passionate commitment and was embodied in such lively characterization and incident that it was possibly more effective than the cooler and more rational arguments put forward by some of the thinkers of the period such as John Henry Newman, Matthew Arnold and Herbert Spencer.

Chapter Nine
Medicine, Doctors, Nurses and Hospitals

Important developments in the world of medicine occurred in the England of the 1850s and after, the period when Dickens was at the height of his powers. The General Medical Council was established in 1858 to regulate the medical profession and to establish a register of qualified practitioners. The use of anaesthetics became widely accepted in the same decade. James Simpson (1811–70) introduced the use of ether and then chloroform in obstetric practice in 1847 – it was administered to Catherine, Dickens's wife, in 1849 at the birth of her eighth child, Henry Fielding Dickens, and to Queen Victoria in 1858 at the birth of her eighth child, Prince Leopold. Joseph Lister (1827–1912), influenced by the discoveries made by Louis Pasteur, pioneered the use of antiseptics in surgery, making use of carbolic acid. Florence Nightingale (1820–1910), following her heroic work as a nurse in the Crimean War (1854–56), did much by her example and writings to reform the administration and conditions of the nursing profession. At the same time as these reforms, sanitary conditions were gradually improved, especially in the towns, after such legislation as the Public Health Act of 1848. Although the death rate fell, life expectancy in 1850 was still only 50. Basic hygienic measures, widespread immunization, X-rays and scans were non-existent and would not be in use until well into the twentieth century. Smallpox was under limited control because of vaccination, but other major diseases (cholera, pneumonia, tuberculosis, diphtheria among them) still threatened the health of everybody. Prince Albert died of typhoid fever in 1861 and the same disease nearly brought about the death of his son, the Prince of Wales, ten years later. People relied on home visits by the family doctor, the surgeon and the midwife for medical attention, if they could afford them.

Given the uncertain nature of medical care compared to what we expect today and given the number of illnesses that were simply accepted as part of everyday life, it is not surprising that Dickens, like other Victorian novelists, presents us with a number of cases of physical and mental incapacity and suffering. According to reputable medical opinion, he is remarkably accurate in dealing with such subjects. John Cosnett, a former physician-neurologist, has stated that 'a feature of Charles Dickens's novels which fascinates physicians is his ability to provide realistic accounts of illnesses and disabilities which affect his characters, with their prominent signs, and sometimes symptoms, accurately portrayed' (Cosnett, 2003, p. 22). Sir Russell Brain, in *Some Reflections on Genius* (1960), also favourably analysed Dickens's presentation of sickness. Among the numerous examples, important for the development of the particular narratives, are the strokes suffered by Mrs Skewton (in *Dombey and Son*) and Sir Leicester Dedlock (in *Bleak House*), the epileptic fits of Monks (in *Oliver Twist*) and Bradley Headstone (in *Our Mutual Friend*), Tiny Tim's tubercular spine, Grandfather Smallweed's paraplegia (in *Bleak House*) and the mental deficiencies of Barnaby Rudge and Maggie (in *Little Dorrit*). Dickens shows sympathy for some of these ailments and diseases, especially when children or simple-minded people are concerned, but at other times we sense that satire, horror, terror or cruelty are uppermost.

Dickens gives us some marvellously inventive black comedy in depicting the worlds of doctors and nurses in the days before the reforms outlined at the beginning of this section. In the *Pickwick Papers* (1837–38), Bob Sawyer and Benjamin Allen, two young medical students, shock the unworldly Mr Pickwick (but amuse Sam Weller) with their happy-go-lucky ways when they are guests of Mr Wardle at Christmas. ' "Nothing like dissecting, to give one an appetite," said Mr Bob Sawyer, looking round the table. Mr Pickwick slightly shuddered.' Jack Hopkins, another medical student, describes the prowess of Mr Slasher, who like other surgeons in those pre-anaesthetic days, had to operate with speed: 'Took a boy's leg out of the socket last week – boy ate five apples and a ginger bread cake – exactly two minutes after it was all over, boy said he wouldn't lie there to be made game of, and he'd tell his mother if they didn't begin' (PP, chs 31, 32). (A few years after writing about operations like this, Dickens himself in October 1841 had a 'cruel operation' performed by Mr Frederick Salmon without an anaesthetic for the alleviation of a rectal fistula.)

Doctor Haggage, the doctor in the Marshalsea Prison where Mr Dorrit and family are incarcerated, is a disreputable practitioner, to say the least, described by Dickens with great relish. He is a prisoner himself and when summoned to attend Mrs Dorrit in childbirth is playing cards, drinking brandy and smoking a pipe with a red-faced and brandy-soaked companion. Haggage was 'amazingly shabby, in a torn and darned rough-weather sea-jacket, out at elbows and eminently short of buttons (he had been in his time the experienced surgeon carried by a passenger ship), the dirtiest white trousers conceivable by mortal man, carpet slippers, and no visible linen.' He immediately agrees to go to the woman in labour – ' "Childbed?" said the doctor. "I'm the boy!"' As soon as the baby (Amy Dorrit) is born, with the assistance of Mrs Bangham, the charwoman and messenger in the prison, he happily returns to his 'associate and chum in hoarseness, puffiness, red-facedness, all-fours [the card game], tobacco, dirt, and brandy' (LD, I, ch. 6).

Mr Chillip, who is supervising the birth of David Copperfield in the comparatively genteel surroundings of Blunderstone Rookery, is in complete contrast to Doctor Haggage but gives the impression of ineffectiveness: 'He was the meekest of his sex, the mildest of little men. He sidled in and out of a room, to take up the less space. He walked as softly as the ghost in *Hamlet*, and more slowly' (DC, ch. 1). The doctors tending Mrs Dombey at the birth of Paul are further up the social scale but are nevertheless unable to save the life of the mother. One of them, Doctor Parker Peps, was 'one of the Court Physicians, and a man of immense reputation for assisting at the increase of great families, [and] was walking up and down the drawing-room with his hands behind him, to the unspeakable admiration of the family Surgeon' (DS, ch. 1). Another physician of high social status is Mr Bayham Badger in *Bleak House*, who has a 'good practice in Chelsea' and who agrees to supervise Richard Carstone's medical studies but again Dickens slyly suggests his inadequacies: he was 'a pink, fresh-faced, crisp-looking gentleman, with a weak voice, white teeth, light hair, and surprised eyes' (BH, ch. 13). He admires his wife on the curious grounds of her having had three husbands.

But in the same novel Dickens depicts an admirable doctor in the person of Allan Woodcourt, who tends Jo and Caddy Jellyby and performs heroic deeds as a ship's surgeon. He marries Esther, who pays him a fulsome tribute at the end of the novel: 'I never lie down at night, but I know that in the course of that day he has alleviated pain, and soothed some fellow-creature in the time of need' (BH, ch. 67). It has to be admitted that Dickens's portrait of Woodcourt is far less inventive, amusing and memorable than his portraits of rascally and incompetent medical practitioners.

The most famous and colourful of all Dickens's medical characters is Mrs Gamp in *Martin Chuzzlewit*. As with Doctor Haggage of the Marshalsea, we have here a depiction which is appalling if taken seriously. But Dickens's linguistic bravura and his imaginative identification with Mrs Gamp make her one of the supreme comic creations in his work – and indeed in English literature. She was a midwife and a 'female functionary, a nurse, and watcher, and performer of nameless offices about the persons of the dead' (MC, ch. 19). John Forster describes her as the 'portentous Mrs Gamp with her grim grotesqueness, her filthy habits and foul enjoyments [mostly drink], her thick and damp but most amazing utterances, her moist clammy functions, her pattens, her bonnet, her bundle, and her umbrella' (Forster, IV, 2). She has an imaginary friend in Mrs Harris and an actual friend in another nurse, Mrs Betsy Prig. They are ruthless in their treatment of patients. When Lewsome, himself a young surgeon, is lying desperately ill, he complains that Mrs Prig put the soap in his mouth when she was washing him. ' "Couldn't you keep it shut then?" retorted Mrs Prig. "Who do you think's to wash one feater, and miss another, and wear one's eyes out with all manner of fine-work of that description, for half-a-crown a day! If you wants to be titivated, you must pay accordin" '(MC, ch. 29). Dickens maintained that he had a serious reforming purpose in presenting readers with the two nurses. In his Preface to the Charles Dickens edition of *Martin Chuzzlewit* (1867), he expressed his hope that in all his writings he had taken

every available opportunity of showing the want of sanitary improvements in the neglected dwellings of the poor [where they would be visited by doctors and nurses]. Mrs Sarah Gamp was, four-and-twenty years ago, a fair representation of the hired attendant on the poor in sickness. The Hospitals of London were, in many respects, noble Institutions; in others, very defective. I think it not the least among their instances of mismanagement, that Mrs Betsy Prig was a fair specimen of a Hospital Nurse; and that the Hospitals, with their means and funds, should have left it to private humanity and enterprise to enter on an attempt to improve that class of persons – since, greatly improved through the agency of good women.

In 'The Hospital Patient', one of the 'characters' in *Sketches by Boz*, written some thirty years before his Preface to *Martin Chuzzlewit*, just quoted, Dickens painted a heart-rending picture of the ward in a London hospital for the poor, with its dim light that 'increased rather than diminished the ghastly appearance of the hapless creatures in the beds, which were ranged in two long rows on either side.' They were victims of accidents and violence, with their faces stamped with the expressions of 'anguish and suffering'. But poor simple-minded Maggy in *Little Dorrit* thinks of the hospital where she was sent as a ten-year-old girl with a 'bad fever' as a blissful place: ' "Such beds there is there!" cried Maggy. "Such lemonades! Such oranges! Such d'licious broth and wine! Such Chicking! Oh, ain't it a delightful place to go and stop at!"' (LD, I, ch. 9). In the same novel, John Baptist Cavaletto, whose leg is broken in a road accident in London, is taken to Saint Bartholomew's Hospital, where the careful surgeon replies to Arthur Clennam's queries 'with the thoughtful pleasure of an artist contemplating the work upon his easel'. Everything is 'skilfully and promptly done.' As 'the lame foreigner with the stick', Cavaletto, after presumably adequate treatment, is made to feel at home in Bleeding House Yard after his discharge from hospital (LD, I, chs. 13, 23).

Dickens made a number of speeches throughout his career in support of those hospitals which as charitable institutions depended on voluntary financial support. To take two examples from the beginning and end of such activities, he spoke on behalf of two London-based institutions: the Hospital for Consumption and Diseases of the Chest on 6 May 1843 and University College Hospital on 12 April 1864. Regarding the first of these hospitals,

Dickens observed that before its foundation in 1842 'poor persons ... would have suffered, lingered, pined, and died in their poor homes, without a hand stretched out to help them in their slow decay' (Fielding, 1988, p. 40). In the later speech, Dickens eloquently appealed for money to be given to the hospital for the medical care it provided, for its services to medical education and for its open-minded refusal to 'coerce the judgement or conscience of any human being' (Fielding, 1988, p. 329).

Chapter Ten
Martin Chuzzlewit, A Christmas Carol, Dombey and Son

Martin Chuzzlewit (1843–44)

The Chuzzlewit family all hope to get their hands on the fortune of old Martin Chuzzlewit, who has as a companion a seventeen-year-old girl named Mary Graham, to whom he has said he will leave no money. His grandson, also named Martin Chuzzlewit, is a complacent and selfish young man, who is a pupil of the hypocritical Mr Pecksniff, an architect and land surveyor and cousin to Martin Chuzzlewit senior. When Pecksniff dismisses him (on old Martin's orders), he goes to America with Mark Tapley. He is duped into investing in worthless land and falls desperately ill. He realizes that his way of life has been selfish, determines to lead a reformed life and returns to England. He eventually wins his grandfather's favour and marries Mary Graham. Jonas Chuzzlewit, old Martin's nephew, is wrongly suspected of murdering Anthony Chuzzlewit, his father, and marries Pecksniff's daugher, Mercy (after leading her sister Charity to believe that she was his wife-to-be). He gets involved with Montague Tigg's fraudulent insurance company, murders Tigg and commits suicide. Pecksniff is ruined by investing in Tigg's company and old Martin exposes him as a hypocrite. In contrast to all these manifestations of selfishness, Dickens presents us with the character of the saintly Tom Pinch, whose sister, Ruth, is also a model of virtue. Dickens ends the novel with a lengthy and grandiloquent apostrophe to Tom. In and out of the narrative appears the unforgettable figure of Mrs Gamp, midwife and nurse, who can justly be called Dickens's greatest comic creation; her utterances are

masterpieces of literary invention in their malapropisms and surrealistic imagery.

Martin Chuzzlewit shows a new development in Dickens's
technique, which up to then had been improvisatory and free and
easy (though *Barnaby Rudge* is something of an exception). In the
Preface to the first edition (1844) he wrote that he had endeav-
oured during its serialization 'to resist the temptation of the current
Monthly Number, and to keep a steadier eye upon the general
purpose and design'. He explained his 'main object' in his Preface to
the first cheap edition (1849): it was 'to exhibit in a variety of aspects
the commonest of all the vices; to show how Selfishness propagates
itself; and to what a grim giant it may grow, from small beginnings'.
The novel was not at first as popular as those that preceded it, and
its American scenes, with their satire on aspects of American life,
aroused anger in the USA. But not long after its first publication it
became widely esteemed as a comic masterpiece, with Pecksniff and
Mrs Gamp as two of the most famous of Dickens's characters.

A Christmas Carol (1843)

Scrooge, a miserly business man, is visited on Christmas Eve by
the ghost of his former partner, Jacob Marley, who tells him he
will be further visited that night by the Ghosts of Christmas Past,
Present and Future. The Ghosts show Scrooge scenes from his youth,
from the imminent Christmas Day and from the future. The most
memorable episode, a blend of humour and pathos, revealed by the
Ghost of Christmas Present, is that of the seasonal celebrations in
the family of Bob Cratchit, Scrooge's poor clerk, whose children
include the poignant figure of Tiny Tim. After these visitations,
Scrooge immediately becomes a reformed man determined to live
a life of love and benevolence – his first action is to order a turkey
to be delivered to the Cratchits. This short book, illustrated by John
Leech and elegantly produced, which made an immediate impact
(the first printing of 6000 copies was sold out in a few days), is easily
the most popular of all Dickens's writings. 'It seems to me a national
benefit', Thackeray wrote in *Fraser's Magazine* in February 1844,
'and to every man or woman who reads it a personal kindness.'

Dickens's other Christmas books and stories are discussed in the 'Christmas' section of this book.

Dombey and Son (1846–48)

Mr Dombey, a cold, proud businessman, is immensely gratified when his son, Paul, is born and is little concerned that his wife dies in giving birth to his heir. He already has a daughter, Florence, but he virtually ignores her as a mere girl. Paul is a sickly child, loved by Florence and his nurse, Polly Toodle. He is sent to Doctor Blimber's school but he dies at the age of six. The loss of Paul is a blow to Mr Dombey's pride and the reader already has a sense of foreboding. Mr Dombey marries a second wife, Edith, who matches him in pride and has married him partly to satisfy her avaricious mother, Mrs Skewton, and partly to find financial security. She eventually runs away to Dijon, where she has arranged to meet James Carker, Mr Dombey's scheming business manager (a melodramatic character). But she contemptuously repels his advances since her only purpose is to humiliate her husband. Realizing that Dombey has tracked him down, Carker flees and is pursued by Dombey back to England, where he is killed by a train (the first fatal railway accident in English fiction – soon to be followed by the death of Captain Brown in Elizabeth Gaskell's *Cranford*). Dombey's shame at the conduct of his wife is succeeded by the collapse of his business, brought about by Carker's machinations. He is a broken man, but after some resistance on his part he is brought to see the truth of the heart's affections, thanks mostly to the newly married Florence, her husband, Walter, and their children.

Alongside the story of the firm of Dombey and Son is a story in a humbler commercial setting. Sol Gills is a ships' instrument maker who faces bankruptcy. His nephew, Walter Gay, works as an office boy in Dombey's firm. Walter rescues Florence from Good Mrs Brown, who has seized her in the street. Dombey, who has condescended to lend Sol Gills some money, is angered by Walter's friendship with Florence. He and Carker therefore send Walter to Barbados on a ship that is later reported missing. Sol Gills goes in search of him, leaving his friend,Captain Cuttle, in charge of the shop. But Walter has survived the shipwreck, returns to England after a long interval, and marries Florence.

Kathleen Tillotson says that *Dombey and Son* 'stands out from among Dickens's novels as the earliest example of responsible and careful planning; it has unity not only of action, but of design and feeling' (Tillotson, 1961, p. 157). The consensus of critical opinion is therefore that the novel 'marks a decisive moment in Dickens's career', as F.R. Leavis states (Leavis and Leavis, 1972, p. 22). John Forster tells us that 'it was to do with Pride what its predecessor [*Martin Chuzzlewit*] had done with Selfishness' (Forster, VI, 2), although he points out that the novel contains much more than that theme alone. Pride, personified above all in Mr Dombey and Edith, is associated with the commercial ethos of the 1840s and is contrasted with the warmth and affection shown in Solomon Gills's household, with the tender goodness of Florence and with the repentance and unselfishness of John Carker, James Carker's brother. The novel has two scenes of powerful emotion: the death of little Paul Dombey, which moved contemporary readers (and Dickens himself) perhaps even more than the death of Little Nell; and the simple wedding of Florence and Walter. Comic characters also abound, including Captain Cuttle, his landlady Mrs McStinger and his friend, Captain Bunsby; the Blimbers who run the school little Paul attends; Major Bagstock; and Mr Toots (a fellow pupil of Paul's at Doctor Blimber's school). But the comedy is less extravagant and hilarious than that in some of Dickens's novels – though Bernard Darwin declared that 'Mr Toots is deathless' (Darwin, 1933, p. 87).

Chapter Eleven
Women and Children

The status of women in English society was frequently discussed in the first half of the nineteenth century. Mary Wollstonecraft's *A Vindication of the Rights of Women* (1792) had been a key publication, although the principal feminist issues did not come to the forefront of public debate until towards the end of Dickens's career. These issues included the rights of married women, divorce, their education, the professions open to them, and the vote – in general, questions of independence, freedom and equality. One step towards liberation was the Matrimonial Causes Act of 1857, which made it theoretically possible (but still difficult) to obtain divorce. But the Married Women's Property Act, which gave women the right to own their own property when they married, was not passed until 1882. Important advances in girls' education were made by Frances Mary Buss, who founded the North London Collegiate School for Girls in 1850 and by Dorothea Beale, who became the headmistress of the Ladies College in Cheltenham in 1858. In the field of further education for women, Girton College, Cambridge, opened in 1869 and Lady Margaret Hall, Oxford, in 1878. Florence Nightingale through her achievements in the Crimean War and her subsequent activities and writings had shown the vital role that could be played by qualified nurses. Elizabeth Garrett Anderson became the first recognized woman doctor in 1865 when she was licensed by the Society of Apothecaries. John Stuart Mill's *The Subjection of Women*, a detailed argument for the equality of the sexes, was published in 1869.

Dickens was ambivalent in his responses to some of the issues relating to the position of women in his time. He encouraged them as authors, publishing work by Elizabeth Gaskell and Adelaide Anne Procter in *Household Words*, his weekly magazine. He was a close associate of the wealthy philanthopist, Angela Burdett Coutts, dedicating *Martin Chuzzlewit* to her and taking an active part in the administration of Urania Cottage, which she had established in 1847 for homeless women. But in *Bleak House* he mocked do-gooders in the persons of Mrs Jellyby, who was more concerned by the plight of Africans than by the management of her own family and who later takes up the cause of the rights of women to sit in Parliament, and Mrs Pardiggle, who was one of those people (according to Mr Jarndyce) 'who did a little and made a great deal of noise' (BH, ch. 8). In 'The Haunted House', one of his *Christmas Stories*, Dickens introduces us to Belinda Bates (modelled on Adelaide Anne Procter), who 'goes in for Woman's rights, Woman's wrongs, and everything that is Woman's with a capital W.' But the narrator of the story whispers a warning to her not to overdo it: although there is a great necessity 'for more employments being within the reach of Woman than our civili-sation has as yet assigned to her, don't fly at the unfortunate men, even those men who are at first sight in your way, as if they were the natural oppressors of your sex; for, trust me, Belinda, they do sometimes spend their wages among wives and daughters, sisters, mothers, aunts and grandmothers, and the play is, really, not all Wolf and Red Riding-Hood, but has other parts in it.'

Dickens, in the variety and complexity of his prolific writing, presents us with all kinds of women, ranging from viragos and dominant wives to meek and mild 'angels in the house'. For his creation of some of these female characters he used traits of the personalities and physical appearance of women he knew, although such influences are often indirect and conjectural. He had important personal relationships of different kinds with eight women: his mother, Elizabeth Dickens; Maria Beadnell, the daughter of a wealthy banker with whom he was passionately in love in the early 1830s; Catherine Hogarth, whom he married in 1836; Mary Hogarth, Catherine's younger sister, whom he also loved but who suddenly died at the age of seventeen; Georgina Hogarth, Catherine's youngest sister, who became Dickens's housekeeper after he and his wife separated; his two daughters, Mary and Kate; and Ellen Ternan, the young actress he met in 1858 and with whom he had an intimate relationship until his death (although the precise nature of the relationship has not been determined). Perhaps influenced by his memories of Mary Hogarth above all, he creates a number of sweet and vapid young women in his early novels: Rose Maylie in *Oliver Twist*, Kate Nickleby in *Nicholas Nickleby* and Mary Graham in *Martin Chuzzlewit* are typical examples.

One young woman of this period is completely different from these Dickensian stereotypes. Nancy in *Oliver Twist*, who belongs to the London criminal world as a prostitute and Bill Sikes's girlfriend, is unprepossessing at first. She and Bet, her companion, call to see the 'young gentlemen' in Fagin's den: 'They wore a good deal of hair: not very neatly turned up behind: and were rather untidy about the shoes and stockings. They were not exactly pretty, perhaps; but they had a great deal of colour in their faces; and looked quite stout and hearty' (OT, ch. 9). But Dickens eventually makes Nancy a sympathetic figure who realizes the error of her ways and whose apparent disloyalty to her criminal associates brings about her brutal murder by Bill Sikes.

Of all the girls and young women in his early fiction, Little Nell in *The Old Curiosity Shop* and Dolly Varden in *Barnaby Rudge* made the deepest impact on contemporary readers. Nellie Trent, the thirteen-year-old girl who accompanies her aged grandfather in his wanderings, is surrounded, as Dickens stated in his 1848 Preface to the novel, with 'grotesque and wild, but not impossible companions' – and hence is similar to Oliver Twist in that respect. Exhausted by her physical ordeals and by her anxieties for her grandfather with his incurable gambling mania, she dies in a country cottage where they have found refuge. As she lay dead, 'she seemed a creature fresh from the hand of God, and waiting for the breath of life' (OCS, ch. 71). Her character and fate led to comparisons with Shakespeare's Cordelia in *King Lear* and Imogen in *Cymbeline*, although today Dickens's portrayal of her is usually dismissed as fulsomely sentimental. Dolly Varden, the daughter of Gabriel Varden the locksmith, is roguish with sparkling eyes; she is 'dimpled, and fresh, and healthful – the very impersonation of youth and blooming beauty' and has 'a thousand little coquettish ways'. She teases her faithful lover, Joe Willet, to distraction but is sorry too late for her flirtatiousness. Held captive during the Gordon Riots, she eventually repents her irresponsible ways and marries Joe. Dickens's description of her 'little straw hat trimmed with cherry-coloured ribbons, and worn the merest trifle on one side' resulted in hats of that sort being named after her (BR, chs. 4, 13, 19). She was so popular as a character that she became the subject of at least four dramatizations of the novel. Dickens himself was so enamoured by his creations of Kate Nickleby and Dolly Varden that he commissioned William Powell Frith to paint their portraits. Intensifying this loving attitude of his, Dickens makes Kate Nickleby, Little Nell and Dolly vulnerable to sexual threats. He clearly suggests that Hugh, the frighteningly coarse hostler at the Maypole Inn, lusts after Dolly just as Sir Mulberry Hawk makes amorous advances to Kate or as the monstrous Quilp threatens the virtue of Little Nell. But Dickens's fond memories of Maria Beadnell inform his delightful portrayal of Dora, David Copperfield's first wife, a loving, childlike and impractical young woman, whom Miss Trotwood affectionately calls 'Little Blossom'. Agnes, always David's guiding spirit, whom he marries after Dora's early death, is as saint-like as her name, but even John Forster found the goodness of this 'angel-wife' hard to take (Forster, VI, 7).

Some of the young women in his middle and later novels are individuals rather than types, since they face particular dilemmas. Esther Summerson, who narrates a half of *Bleak House*, is sometimes derided by critics as impossibly unselfish and naïve since, in John Forster's words, we find her 'artlessly unconscious' (Forster, VII, 1) of some of the things that happen to her. But Dickens's rendering of her quiet and consistent nature and her capacity for love form a positive and rewarding counterbalance to the intrigues and deceits that figure in the third-person narrative. The frustrations of Louisa Gradgrind in *Hard Times*, the cold disdain of Estella for Pip and all men in *Great Expectations*, Bella Wilfer's love for her father blended with her avowed mercenary nature in *Our Mutual Friend*, Lizzie Hexam's determined practicality and her despairing (but eventually fulfilled) love for Eugene Wrayburn (also in *Our Mutual Friend*) have a convincing realism far removed from the caricatures for which Dickens is conventionally reprehended.

Similar in some respects are the women tortured by disappointment and anger – prominent among these are Rosa Dartle, who has harboured an unfulfilled love for Steerforth in *David Copperfield*, and Miss Wade, who recounts her own 'History of a Self-Tormentor' in *Little Dorrit*. Miss Wade encourages Tattycoram, the resentful girl adopted and patronized by the Mr and Mrs Meagles, to run away from their well-meaning care and to live with her for a while. Edith Dombey, Mr Dombey's second wife, is consumed by self-abasement that jars against her pride. She is to a large extent a melodramatic and stagey creation, as shown in Phiz's magnificent image of her in the plate captioned 'Mr Carker in his Hour of Triumph', but Dickens's rhetoric, displayed in her passionate speeches, generates a formidable power. Nevertheless, exaggeration of the most entertaining kind colours his portraits of sharp-tongued women who dominate their households: Mrs Varden in *Barnaby Rudge*, who has a spiteful coadjutor in Miss Miggs, the maidservant; Mrs Gargery who in *Great Expectations* exercises supreme power over Joe Gargery, her husband, and who boasts that she has brought up Pip 'by hand'; and Mrs Wilfer who is loftily superior to everyone including her gentle husband, R.W. Wilfer, in *Our Mutual Friend*.

Dickens enjoys presenting us with young women who may seem pathetic at first sight but who are stronger than the men in their lives: in *The Old Curiosity Shop*, the downtrodden servant girl, the Marchioness, tends to Dick Swiveller in his fever and, in the same novel, Little Nell takes charge of her grandfather; in *Our Mutual Friend*, Jenny Wren, the crippled dolls' dressmaker, has to watch over her drunken father, her 'troublesome bad child'. Eccentrics and grotesques abound: Mrs Gamp in *Martin Chuzzlewit*; Mrs Nickleby, whose rambling and surrealistic reminiscences are apparently based on Dickens's mother's conversation; Miss Flite in *Bleak House*, with her obsession with the Court of Chancery and her symbolically named cage birds; the frightening Mr F.'s Aunt, who accompanies Flora Finching and who utters cryptic and surrealistic remarks in *Little Dorrit*; the weird Miss Havisham, clad in her decaying wedding gown, who is an inescapable and baleful influence on Estella and Pip in *Great Expectations*; Miss Mowcher, the dwarf manicurist and hairdresser who regularly attends to Steerforth in *David Copperfield*. Three formidable women, out of a large number, are Mrs Sparsit, Mr Bounderby's housekeeper in *Hard Times*; Mrs General, engaged by Mr Dorrit after his release from prison to instruct his two daughters, Amy (Little Dorrit) and Fanny, in suitably genteel conversation and behaviour, advising them to practise saying 'prunes and prism' as 'very good words for the lips' (LD, II, ch. 5); and Miss Pross, Lucy Manette's indomitably patriotic companion in *A Tale of Two Cities*.

Dickens wrote three books for children, although these are infrequently read. He wrote *The Life of Our Lord* (originally entitled *The Children's New Testament*) in 1846 for reading aloud to his children but not for publication. It did not appear in print until 1934. His *Child's History of England* (first serialized in *Household Words* between January 1851 and December 1853) goes up to 1688 only (the year of the Glorious Revolution). *A Holiday Romance*, published simultaneously in Britain and the USA in 1868, consists of four stories, each narrated by a child. None of these three books can be called major achievements (though *A Holiday Romance* has its delights), but children are especially – and unusually – important characters in Dickens's work. The memories of his own childhood, especially of the period he spent as a twelve-year-old in Warren's Blacking Warehouse, haunted him throughout his life. He had other recollections that were both enjoyable and disturbing. In 'Where We Stopped Growing', an autobiographical piece published in *Household Words* on 1 January 1853, he recalls his childhood delight in certain books (*Robinson Crusoe* and the *Arabian Nights* among them) – a delight that was also evoked in *David Copperfield*. He remembers in the same essay attractive and forbidding people, places and buildings in London – one of those buildings was, significantly, Newgate Prison. As well as these memories of his boyhood, his sympathies as an adult observer were aroused by the pitiful condition of the many poor children (like Jo in *Bleak House* and those who appear anonymously here and there in *Sketches by Boz*) he saw around him in the London streets and whose plight was a frequent subject of discussion and action among Victorian philanthropists and legislators (such as Lord Shaftesbury). Although Tiny Tim in *A Christmas Carol* lives in an affectionate and caring household, his disability as a cripple has made him vulnerable, especially since the Cratchits are so poor. The wretched Smike, whom Nicholas Nickleby rescues from the clutches of Squeers, highlights the helpless state of the boys sent away to the Yorkshire boarding schools.

Dickens used child characters to represent innocence and goodness, including Little Nell (as we saw above) and Oliver Twist, both of whom find themselves surrounded by threatening and cruel people and circumstances. Paul Dombey, who is nevertheless fully realized as a credible little boy, has an instinctive knowledge of what is truly valuable in the materialistic world in which he finds himself. When he asks Mr Dombey, who is a business man obsessed with the prosperity of his business firm, what money is after all, his father is nonplussed, gazing 'with sheer amazement at the presumptuous atom that propounded such an inquiry'. Paul is puzzled by Mr Dombey's assertion that money can do almost anything since (as he says) it failed to save his mother from death and cannot make him 'strong and quite well' (DS, ch. 8). The small boy, subjected to the strict tuition of Mrs Pipchin (whom he can nevertheless disconcert) and Doctor Blimber's school, finds happiness and contentment in his dreams, in Old Glubb's fantastic stories and in his visions on his deathbed. In *Hard Times*, Louisa and Tom Gradgrind, the children of the strictly rational Mr Gradgrind (who is like Mr Dombey to some extent), hunger for the delights of Mr Sleary's travelling circus and peep through a fence to see what they can, much to their father's astonishment and anger: 'I should as soon have expected to see my children reading poetry' (HT, I, ch. 4). Barnaby Rudge, though in his early twenties, is simple and childlike and finds delight in sights like clouds of smoke going up the chimney and stars with angels' eyes. He has an untutored imagination far removed from the religious fanaticism of the Gordon rioters with whom he becomes unwittingly and dangerously involved.

As in his opinions on education, Dickens asserts through these children and childhood figures the power of fancy as well as goodness, echoing, consciously or unconsciously, the views associated with Rousseau (as in *Emile*, his novel that propounded imaginative approaches to children's education) and Wordsworth (whose poem, 'We are Seven', was one of Dickens's favourites). A few impertinent boys make comic appearances although not so many as might be expected in those days when John Leech drew so many of them in *Punch* and elsewhere and when a number of them look cheekily out of the background to some of Phiz's illustrations. Trabb's boy in *Great Expectations* (a character particularly admired by G.K. Chesterton), 'the most audacious boy in all that countryside', mocks Pip's pretensions when they meet in the street (GE, ch. 19) and Deputy (also known as Winks), 'a hideous small boy', is paid a halfpenny by

Durdles in *The Mystery of Edwin Drood* 'to pelt him home' if he is out late (MED, ch. 5). Mrs Pocket, in *Great Expectations*, relies on her two nursemaids to control her seven children, as she is as ineffective in household matters as Mrs Jellyby in *Bleak House*. Pip is made very uneasy in his mind by 'Mrs Pocket's falling into a discussion with Drummle respecting two baronetcies while she ate a sliced orange steeped in sugar and wine, and forgetting all about the baby on her lap; who did most appalling things with the nutcrackers', which have be coaxed away by Jane, one of his little sisters (GE, ch. 23).

Dickens's most telling evocations of childhood are those in two first-person narratives: *David Copperfield* and *Great Expectations*. David's affections, fears and precise observation have the ring of truth, suggesting that Dickens's own experiences, sometimes transformed into wishful thinking or wistful recollection, lie behind them. He remembers the store room at Blunderstone Rookery, ' in which there is the smell of soap, pickles, pepper, candles, and coffee'; Peggotty, his nurse, squeezing him so tight in her affection for him that two buttons burst from her gown to 'the opposite side of the parlour'; Mr Murdstone with his 'ill-omened black eyes'; David's young mother eager to hear of the flattering remarks made about her beauty, 'kneeling down playfully by the side of the bed, and laying her chin upon her hands, and laughing' (DC, ch. 2). Truthfulness of sensuous recollection is combined with honesty of characterization, since young David is resilient and tough (as young Charles Dickens was). He bites through Mr Murdstone's hand when his stepfather is caning him --a memory that sets his teeth on edge when he thinks about it. After Mr Creakle, his headmaster, tells him that his mother is dead, he is grief-stricken but stands on a chair when he is left alone and 'looked into the glass to see how red my eyes were, and how sorrowful my face.' He admits that his grief gave him an importance among his schoolfellows and that when he knew they were looking at him he felt distinguished, 'and looked more melancholy, and walked slower' (DC, ch. 9).

Pip in *Great Expectations* has frightening and puzzling experiences, scared by the escaped convict, bullied by his sister and other adults at the Christmas dinner and treated with disdain by Estella in the ghostly surroundings of Salem House. But he mischievously lies to Mrs Gargery, Joe and Uncle Pumblechook about what he saw on his first visit to Miss Havisham. He tells them, with what we can truly call Dickensian invention, that she was sitting in 'a black velvet coach' and that everyone ate 'cake and wine on gold plates' (GE, ch. 9). On his next visit, Pip, when the 'pale young gentleman' (later identified as Herbert Pocket) challenges him to a fight, continually knocks him down. These two boys, David Copperfield and Pip, have a reality, founded upon a combination of worthy and occasionally unworthy qualities, that contrasts with the partly allegorical function of children like Oliver Twist, Little Nell and Florence Dombey.

Chapter Twelve
Dickens and Animals

John Forster wrote that 'Dickens's interest in dogs (as in the habits and ways of all animals) was inexhaustible, and he welcomed with delight any new trait [of their behaviour]' (Forster, VIII, 3). His dogs were mostly big powerful animals, including Turk (of 'the mastiff kind'), Linda (a St Bernard), Sultan (a cross between a St Bernard and a bloodhound, who turned out to be so aggressive that he had to be killed), Don (a Newfoundland) and two more Newfoundlands. Mamie, his elder daughter, owned a 'handsome little Pomeranian', called Mrs Bouncer. When Dickens's pet raven died in 1841, it was replaced by another, 'so that *Barnaby [Rudge]* should have the fruit of continued study of the habits of the family of birds which Grip [in that novel] had so nobly represented' (Forster, II, ch. 9). Dickens enthusiastically expressed his near anthropomorphic delight in his pet animals in letters to his friends. To give two examples: he gave a long account, with comic detail, of his raven's death in a letter of 12 March 1841 to Daniel Maclise, the artist, and in 1868 he told Mrs James T. Fields, the wife of the American publisher, of the emotional way two of his Newfoundland dogs greeted him on his return from the USA (Letters, II, pp. 230–2; XII, pp. 118–20).

Animals and birds, with marked identities and idiosyncrasies, appear in Dickens's fiction, sometimes because he simply enjoys depicting them and at other times because he uses them to enhance characteristics of their owners and the atmosphere of a scene or story. Grip, Barnaby Rudge's pet raven, a 'compound of two great originals' in Dickens's 'proud possession', according to his Preface to the novel, is a menacing and knowing presence in a world of secret murder, fanaticism and violence. Dickens explained his intention in a letter of 28 January 1841 to George Cattermole, one of the two illustrators of *Barnaby Rudge*: 'Barnaby being an idiot my notion is to have him always in company with a pet raven who is immeasurably more knowing than himself' (Letters, II, p. 197). Grip can speak, and his first utterance in the story proclaims his mischievous and diabolical character: 'Halloa, halloa, halloa! What's the matter here? Keep up your spirits. Never say die. Bow bow bow. I'm a devil, I'm a devil, I'm a devil. Hurrah!' (BR, ch. 6). At a melancholy meeting of Barnaby, his mother, Mr Haredale and his niece, the raven 'with the air of some old necromancer appeared to be profoundly studying a great folio volume that lay open on a desk, was strictly in unison with the rest [of the company], and looked like the embodied Spirit of Evil biding his time of mischief' (BR, ch. 25). Grip survives everything despite temporarily losing his power of speech because of the sufferings he and Barnaby have undergone during and after the Gordon Riots. Dickens, in recognition of the raven's apparent near immortality, devotes the last words of the novel to him: 'he has very probably gone on talking to the present time.' Edgar Allan Poe, who reviewed *Barnaby Rudge* when it first appeared, had Grip in mind when he wrote his best-known poem, 'Nevermore'.

Dickens makes use of an even more frightening creature in *Bleak House*. Lady Jane, Krook's large grey cat, is as rapacious and menacing as her master, leaping down and ripping at a bundle of rags 'with her tigerish claws, with a sound that it set [Esther Summerson's] teeth on edge to hear'. Miss Flite, who sees Lady Jane as a threat to her twenty caged larks, linnets and goldfinches, sometimes half believes that 'she is no cat, but the wolf of the old saying. It is so very difficult to keep her from the door.' The cat 'expands her wicked mouth and snarls' at Mr Tulkinghorn when he visits Krook and later snarls again at the 'crumbled black thing on the floor', which is all that remains of Krook after his appalling death by means of spontaneous combustion (BH, chs. 5, 10, 32). Phiz, who achieved some of his finest visual effects in his illustrations to *Bleak House*, puts Lady Jane into two of the pictures: in one, the cat is perched on Krook's shoulders when he chalks letters on the wall for Esther to see and, in the other, she stands with tail erect confronting Krook's remains as Guppy and Jopling look at it with horror.

The wretchedness and violence of the criminal life in London in the 1830s are evident in Dickens's description of Bill Sikes's dog, Bull's-eye, white and shaggy, 'with his face scratched and torn in twenty different places' (OT, ch. 13). He skulks in Fagin's den, cowed by Sikes, who kicks him to the other end of the room. On his second appearance, he savagely turns on Sikes and like his master struggles and utters aggressive noises. Later, he seems anxious to 'attach himself' to Oliver Twist's windpipe when Sikes and Nancy recapture the little boy (OT, ch. 16). When Sikes, having accidentally hanged himself in his panic-stricken attempt to escape his pursuers, is dangling from the chimney, Bull's-eye tries to jump for the dead man's shoulders, misses his aim, falls, strikes his head against a stone and dashes out his brains. The macabre appropriateness of the dog's death is a clinching recognition of the murderous and yet pitiful existences that preceded it.

Dickens must have been thinking of his own dogs when in *Little Dorrit* he depicted Henry Gowan's 'fine Newfoundland dog' named Lion (a name probably suggested by his friend Edwin Landseer's 1823 painting, *Lion, a Newfoundland Dog*). When Gowan is painting a portrait in Venice of the sinister adventurer, Blandois (also known as Rigaud), Little Dorrit is so fearfully attracted by Blandois's 'peculiar eyes' that she cannot remove her own. At the same time, Lion, somehow provoked by Blandois, is violently resolved to attack him, despite Gowan's seizing him by the collar. Gowan furiously orders Blandois out of the room, shouting that the dog will kill him, and then fells Lion with a blow to the head and kicks him 'many times severely with the heel of his boot'. He spares him further punishment when Little Dorrit intercedes and Dickens comments (again with his own experiences with dogs in mind) that 'he was as submissive, and as sorry, and as wretched as a dog could be' (LD, II, ch. 6). A few days later, Gowan's wife (the former Pet Meagles) whispers to Little Dorrit that Blandois killed the dog, something that Little Dorrit thinks is true. Blandois, whose subtle machinations have just been made clear again, has told Henry Gowan that Lion was already poisoned when the dog tried to attack him. Lion is an embodiment of Gowan's reserves of anger and Blandois's ruthlessness.

Diogenes and Jip, the pet dogs of Florence Dombey and Dora (in *David Copperfield*), are presented by Dickens with liveliness and affection. Diogenes (whose classical name was given him by the pedantic teachers and school proprietors, the Blimbers, his first owners) is 'a blundering, ill-favoured, clumsy, bullet-headed dog'

(DS, ch. 18) who is a lively creature, present on many occasions with his young mistress. Dickens indulges at one point in a remarkable apostrophe, when Diogenes barks at the threatening figure of Mr Carker, who has designs on Florence: 'Well spoken, Di, so near your Mistress! Another, and another with your head up, your eyes flashing, and your vexed mouth worrying itself, for want of him! Another, as he picks his way along! You have a good scent, Di – cats, boy, cats!' (DS, ch. 22). Dora, David Copperfield's girl-wife, is inseparable from the yapping and demanding Jip, who lives in a little pagoda, tears the pages of her cookery book and must have a mutton chop every day (or else, she says, he will die) – but he growls and howls in the presence of Miss Trotwood. At Dora's death, he 'lies down at [David Copperfield's] feet, stretches himself out as if to sleep, and with a plaintive cry, is dead' (DC, ch. 53).

Other animals that Dickens lovingly depicts are Whisker, the Garlands' 'obstinate-looking, rough-coated pony' who becomes meek and tractable in Kit Nubbles's hands (OCS, ch. 38); Merrylegs, Signor Jupe's performing dog in *Hard Times* whose death in front of Mr Sleary indicates that his missing master has also died; and Dick, Tim Linkinwater's blind blackbird, which he keeps in a cage in the Brothers Cheeryble's counting house in *Nicholas Nickleby*.

Chapter Thirteen
David Copperfield, Bleak House

David Copperfield (1849–50)

David Copperfield, who tells his own story, begins disarmingly: 'Whether I shall turn out to be the hero of my own life, or whether that station will be held by anybody else, these pages must show.' As a small boy, he lives at Blunderstone Rookery with his loving young widowed mother and her affectionate servant, Peggotty. Peggotty takes him to stay with her family at Yarmouth and on his return home he finds that his mother has remarried. His stepfather, Mr Murdstone, and Murdstone's sister immediately take charge of the household. Murdstone treats David with unyielding sternness and when he beats him for not knowing his lessons David bites through his hand. David is sent away to Mr Creakle's school, Salem House, where he becomes acquainted with Steerforth and Tommy Traddles. But when his mother dies he has to leave school and go to work at Murdstone and Grinby's warehouse in London, lodging with the Micawber family. When Mr Micawber is arrested for debt, David makes his way to Dover, where he is taken in by Miss Trotwood, his great-aunt, who already looks after the simple-minded, kindly Mr Dick, and who becomes an acute and benevolent adviser to David in all his doings. She sends him to Doctor Strong's admirable school in Canterbury, where he lives with Mr Wickfield, a lawyer, and Agnes, his daughter. David eventually becomes a parliamentary reporter and novelist. He marries Dora, his delightful but impractical wife, although there is no doubt that Agnes Wickfield truly loves him as well.

Tragedies and crises befall many of the people he knows. Emily, Mr Peggotty's niece, is seduced by Steerforth. After Mr Peggotty has long searched for her abroad, David and he find her in London, with the help of Martha, a prostitute. Repentant, she is restored to the care of Mr Peggotty, who decides to take her to Australia to begin a new life there. Ham Peggotty, who had always loved Emily, is drowned in a great storm at Yarmouth while trying unsuccessfully to rescue a sailor, who ironically turns out to be Steerforth. Uriah Heep, Mr Wickfield's clerk, begins to take control of the lawyer's business and schemes to marry Agnes but his evil doings are unmasked by Mr Micawber in a memorable confrontation. After Dora dies, David marries Agnes. The Micawbers, like the Peggotty family, emigrate to Australia. Other notable characters are Mr Barkis, the carrier, who marries Peggotty but dies (going 'out with the tide') before the story is over; the middle-aged Doctor Strong, his young wife, Annie, and Mrs Markleham, his mother-in-law; Mrs Steerforth, the proud mother of James, and her companion, Miss Dartle; the dwarf, Miss Mowcher, a manicurist and hairdresser; Littimer, Steerforth's manservant; and Mrs Gummidge, who lives in the Peggotty household.

David Copperfield has elements of autobiography, including Dickens's boyhood reading, the likenesses between his father and Mr Micawber, Dickens's experiences in Warren's Blacking Warehouse, and his early days as a reporter and up-and-coming novelist. But John Forster's words are salutary: 'it would be the greatest mistake to imagine anything like a complete identity of the fictitious novelist with the real one, beyond the Hungerford scenes [in and around Warren's warehouse]' (Forster, VI, 7). Nevertheless, in his Preface to the 'Charles Dickens' edition, Dickens wrote that 'like many fond parents, I have in my heart of hearts a favourite child. And his name is David Copperfield.' It was Dickens's first novel to be written in the first person and its prose style has an ease and directness that convey a feeling of sincere and actual experience. The narrative is interrupted by four 'Retrospects', in which David blends pictures, doubts and hopes as he recalls different stages of his life. We can turn to Forster again for a Victorian evaluation of the novel's fundamental message: from its profusion of events and characters 'we learn the value of self-denial and patience, quiet endurance of unavoidable ills, strenuous effort against ills remediable; and everything in the fortunes of the actors warns us, to strengthen our generous emotions and to guard the purities of home' (Forster, VI, 7). Worth noting is the fact that it was published at the same time as other imaginative works based on autobiography: Thackeray's *Pendennis* (1848–50), Wordsworth's poem, *The Prelude* (in its final, posthumous version, 1850), Tennyson's sequence of poems, *In Memoriam* (1850), and Charlotte Bronte's *Villette* (1853). Along with the *Pickwick Papers*, *David Copperfield* has always been the most popular of Dickens's novels, mainly for the reasons that Forster gave.

Bleak House (1852–53)

The novel is equally divided between two narrators, whose stories run side by side: Esther Summerson, who confides in the reader using the first person and the past tense, and the omniscient third-person narrator who writes in the present tense. The prolonged law suit of Jarndyce v. Jarndyce in the Court of Chancery is central to the activities, identities and fortunes of the main characters although its ramifications are a puzzle to everyone involved in it. Ada Clare and Richard Carstone, two wards in the case, have come to live in Bleak House, under the kindly guardianship of Mr Jarndyce, who employs Esther as a companion to Ada and as his housekeeper. In the parallel narrative, Sir Leicester and his wife, Lady Dedlock, who live in Chesney Wold, Lincolnshire, are visited by Mr Tulkinghorn, their lawyer, who brings them mysterious but disturbing news about the Jarndyce suit. Mr Guppy, a lawyer's clerk, becomes infatuated with Esther but she rejects his advances. Having seen a portrait of Lady Dedlock, he eventually guesses that she is Esther's mother, a secret that Tulkinghorn has also discovered. When Tulkinghorn is shot dead at his house, suspicion falls on Trooper George (the owner of a shooting gallery) and Lady Dedlock, but Inspector Bucket (one of the first police detectives in English fiction) proves that the murder was committed by Hortense, Lady Dedlock's maid. Lady Dedlock is found dead at the gates of the cemetery where her lover, Captain Hawdon, the father of Esther, is buried. Esther has become disfigured as a result of smallpox, caught from her devoted maid, Charley, who in turn had nursed the pathetic Jo, a crossing-sweeper, who dies from the disease. Ada secretly marries the feckless Richard, who dies soon afterwards, broken in spirit and health because of the frustrations he had experienced regarding the Jarndyce v. Jarndyce. Mr Jarndyce releases Esther from her engagement to him so that she is free to marry the young surgeon, Allan Woodcourt. Among other people involved somehow or other in legal entanglements are Miss Flite, the Smallweed family, Krook (a dealer in junk, ironically nicknamed the Lord Chancellor), Skimpole (based on Leigh Hunt), Boythorn (based on Walter Savage Landor), Mrs Jellyby , the Turveydrops and Mr Chadband.

Besides his primary purpose of exposing and satirizing the Court of Chancery and the legal system, Dickens portrays social evils and shortcomings of England in the middle of the nineteenth century: the condition of the poorest classes, political inefficiency and corruption, the prevalence of dirt and disease (including smallpox), and overcrowded burial grounds. His graphic scene of Krook's death by 'spontaneous combustion' excited controversy. George Henry Lewes attacked the phenomenon as non-scientific although Dickens continued to defend its existence as a proven fact in his Prefaces to editions of the novel.

Bleak House is often classified as the first of Dickens's so-called 'dark novels'. G.K. Chesterton thought that it represented 'the highest point of his intellectual maturity' but that it was not certainly his 'best book' (Chesterton, 1933, p. 148). But sweetness,virtue and benevolence exist (embodied in the depiction of Esther Summerson and in Mr Jarndyce) along with humour, as in all of Dickens's novels, despite the existence of so many tragic elements and its deeply felt social messages. Dickens concluded his Prefaces, mentioned above, with a brief but important statement of his literary art: 'In *Bleak House*, I have purposely dwelt upon the romantic side of familiar things.'

Chapter Fourteen
Dickens's Comic Characters and Villains

Early readers prized Dickens's comic powers above all. John Forster wrote that Dickens's 'leading quality was Humour', which accounted 'for his magnificent successes, as well as for his not infrequent failures, in characteristic delineation'. Forster went on to quote from a letter that Dickens wrote in 1865 to Bulwer-Lytton, one of his fellow novelists: 'I have such an inexpressible enjoyment of what I see in a droll light, that I dare say I pet it as if it were a spoilt child' (Forster, IX, 1). The line between comic characters and villains in Dickens's work is sometimes a fine one. Mr Jingle, in *Pickwick Papers*, is primarily a comic figure but he is a scheming rogue. Quilp, in *The Old Curiosity Shop*, is monstrous and terrifying but Dickens writes about him in a spirit of grotesque humour.

The most famous and original of Dickens's primarily comic personages are to be found in the novels he wrote in the earlier part of his career, i.e., those from *Pickwick Papers* to *David Copperfield*. The later novels, with their more serious intent and with their darker and grimmer elements, do not lend themselves so readily to the creation of comic characters, although they never disappear completely from Dickens's fiction. In *A Tale of Two Cities* Jerry Cruncher, for example, provides some lighter moments though he lacks the sparkle of earlier roguish characters. At the beginning of Dickens's career, humorous characters were popular in fiction and light verse. As was said in the first section of this book, he was writing in the same mode as Thomas Hood, R.H. Barham (in the *Ingoldsby Legends*), Theodore Hook, Douglas Jerrold and the young Thackeray, though there was little or no sign of imitation. The stories in *Sketches by Boz* abound in amusing men and women, signified by their names, which from the beginning carry the authentic Dickensian stamp: Augustus Minns, the Tuggses, Horatio Sparkins and Watkins Tottle, to name a few of them.

The appearance of Sam Weller, who becomes Mr Pickwick's manservant, in the fourth monthly instalment of *Pickwick Papers* was the starting-point for the novel's amazing success. The resourceful servant was a conventional figure in picaresque novels and dramas of intrigue: Sancho Panza in Cervantes' *Don Quixote* and Figaro, the barber, in Beaumarchais' plays are the two most famous examples in world literature. Among Dickens's predecessors, Tobias Smollett had created Strap in *Roderick Random* (1748) and Henry Fielding had created Partridge (naïve rather than sharp-witted) in *Tom Jones* (1749), two novels that Dickens had read as a boy. But Dickens gave Sam Weller a high-spirited Cockney sharpness, wit and irrepressibility that readers had never before encountered, expressed in colloquial London talk (with the letters 'v' and 'w' often transposed) that is full of anecdotes, similes and advice – a mixture such as Shakespeare might have written for his servants and lower-class people. The word, 'Wellerism', has had to be invented to describe this character's unique mode of speech. Much quoted examples include 'Avay with melincholly, as the little boy said ven his school missis died', 'Out vith it, as the father said wen he swallowed a farden', and 'Anythin' for a quiet life, as the man said wen he took the sitivation at the lighthouse.' The black humour – fun made of death, illness and sadness – so concisely expressed reminds us that Dickens was writing in 1836–37, before the Victorian age had really begun, when propriety and decorum would have inhibited any suggestion of callousness. Sam is always at hand to rescue or defend the hapless Mr Pickwick and is unfailingly optimistic. He is unabashed by the severe Mr Stareleigh and the bullying Serjeant Buzfuz at the trial of Bardell v. Pickwick. When Buzfuz cannot believe that he did not see what went on between Mrs Bardell and Mr Pickwick in Mrs Bardell's house and asks him whether he has a pair of eyes, he answers 'without the slightest appearance of irritation': ' "Yes, I have a pair of eyes … and that's just it. If they wos a pair o' patent double million magnifyin' gas microscopes of hextra power, p'raps I might be able to see through a flight o' stairs and a deal door; but bein' only eyes, you see, my wision is limited" ' (PP, ch. 34). Tony Weller, his father, amused Dickens's readers as well, with his amiable nature and philosophizing. Dickens, realizing their popularity, briefly but unmemorably resurrected the Wellers (and Mr Pickwick) in *Master Humphrey's Clock*.

Dickens conceives Sam Weller in the medium of a particular mode of English language – the speech you could hear in the London streets but with Dickens's own heightening of its idioms. But he deploys these words and expressions with a casual naturalness far removed from the more conscious methods of Pierce Egan, whose *Life in London* (1821) had been a sensational success. In the *Pickwick Papers* Dickens uses a distinctive verbal pattern for Mr Jingle, a strolling player and a happy-go-lucky opportunist with pretensions. Without their particular modes of speech, both Sam Weller and Mr Jingle are much diminished. Jingle's staccato speech was a trick that had been used by other writers, including Dickens's close friend Captain Marryat for his character of Cophagus in *Japhet in Search of a Father*, but Dickens brings his remarkable inventiveness to bear in such remarks as Jingle's definition of Kent: 'Kent, sir – everybody knows Kent – apples, cherries, hops, and women.' Jingle, like Sam Weller, can tell cruel anecdotes, as when he and the Pickwickians are travelling by coach to Rochester: ' " Heads, heads – take care of your heads!" cried the loquacious stranger, as they came out under the low archway, which in those days formed the entrance to the coachyard. "Terrible place – dangerous work – other day – five children – mother – tall lady, eating sandwiches – forgot the arch – crash – knock – children look round – no mouth to put it in – head of a family off – shocking, shocking!" ' (PP, ch. 2).

Dickens's enthusiasm for the stage finds a personification in Vincent Crummles, the actor-manager of a travelling troupe of actors, whom Nicholas Nickleby and Smike meet as they make their way towards Portsmouth. Mr Crummles thinks they have the potential to be actors: ' "There's genteel comedy in your walk and manner, juvenile tragedy in your eye, and touch-and-go farce in your laugh," said Mr Vincent Crummles [to Nicholas]. "You'll do as well as if you had thought of nothing else but the lamps, from your birth downwards"' (NN, ch. 22). When Nicholas announces his intention of leaving the company, Mr Crummles insists that he make three 'last' appearances and wonders whether as a novelty act he could sing 'a comic song on the pony's back' (NN, ch. 30). Dickens based

Mr Crummles and his family (including his daughter, the so-called Infant Phenomenon) on a well-known actor of the time, Thomas Donald Davenport, and his daughter, Jean, but again, as with the literary prototypes of Sam Weller and Alfred Jingle in the *Pickwick Papers*, he endows them with an individuality and eccentricity of his own making. Crummles can also be seen as an embodiment of the theatricality that has often been seen to pervade *Nicholas Nickleby*.

Dick Swiveller in *The Old Curiosity Shop* (a rogue Dickens transforms into a sympathetic young man as the story unfolds) is also a theatrical creation with a distinctive mode of speech, marked by flowery expressions and quotations from popular songs: ' "Fred," said Mr Swiveller [to Little Nell's brother], "remember the once popular melody of 'Begone dull care'; fan the sinking flame of hilarity with the wing of friendship: and pass the rosy wine!"' (OCS, ch. 7), He is little regarded today – readers prefer the uneasily strange characterizations and encounters that one experiences in *The Old Curiosity Shop* – but Margaret Oliphant, the novelist who wrote a critical article on Dickens in *Blackwood's Magazine* in April 1855, ranked him with Sam Weller as a 'distinct and true' person (Collins, 1971, p. 331), and J.B. Priestley, as we have seen, wrote an appreciation of him.

Two more comic figures (out of many) that deserve comment have different functions in the novels where they appear. Dickens was following the tradition of Ben Jonson (whose plays he knew well) and others in making Mr Pecksniff, an architect and land surveyor in *Martin Chuzzlewit*, a representative of a particular 'humour' – Pecksniff is the incarnation of hypocrisy. John Forster confirms this when he says that 'no conceivable position, action, or utterance find him without the vice in which his being is wholly steeped and saturated' (Forster, IV, 2). The 'vice' can be considered as an aspect of the theme of selfishness, which Dickens proclaimed in his Preface as the subject of *Martin Chuzzlewit*. Sam Weller, Mr Jingle, Mr Crummles and Dick Swiveller radiate exuberance and a kind of joy among the company they keep, but Pecksniff is unappealing to say the least in his relationship with others, although Dickens's satire is pointed and comic. He tells us directly that Pecksniff was 'a most exemplary man: fuller of virtuous precept than a copy-book' with a 'person' that was 'sleek though free from corpulence' and a manner that was 'soft and oily' (MC, ch. 2). Dickens consistently has this key appraisal in mind. It can appear in a phrase: after being disconcerted for a moment, Mr Pecksniff recovered 'from his surprise, and was in full possession of his virtuous self'. It can appear in subtle touches in a conversation. When Mrs Todgers, who effusively welcomes Mr Pecksniff and his daughters, Charity and Mercy, to her London lodging-house after several years have gone by, she exclaims that he is 'not a bit changed':

> 'What do you say to this?' cried Mr Pecksniff, stretching out his hand towards the young ladies. 'Does this make me no older?'
>
> 'Not your daughters!' exclaimed the lady, raising her hands and clasping them. 'Oh, no, Mr Pecksniff! Your second [wife], and her bridesmaid!'
>
> Mr Pecksniff smiled complacently; shook his head; and said, 'My daughters, Mrs Todgers. Merely my daughters.' (MC, ch. 8)

Dickens uses a soliloquy when Pecksniff condescendingly visits Ruth Pinch, the sister of Tom Pinch, his devoted assistant (who cannot see through Pecksniff's hypocrisy), making him imagine that he speaks to her in the following words: 'You see in me, young person, the benefactor of your race; the patron of your house; the preserver of your brother, who is fed with manna daily from my table; and in right of whom there is a considerable balance in my favour at present standing in the books beyond the sky. But I have no pride, for I can afford to do without it!' (MC, ch. 9). Dickens cannot allow Pecksniff to succeed and so satisfies his readers with contriving his exposure and downfall, brought so low that he is forced to borrow money from Tom Pinch. Most people would agree with the claim that Dickens glories in his portrayal of Pecksniff, although some may have their reservations, insisting that his conception is narrowed by the 'humour' that he makes Pecksniff personify.

But nobody can doubt Dickens's enthusiasm in his portrayal of Mr Micawber in *David Copperfield*. Like Pecksniff, Mr Micawber has become a byword. *Chambers Dictionary* defines 'Micawberish' as 'jaunty and improvident, always "waiting for something to turn up"'. But Micawber is too full-blooded to be regarded simply as the personification of a 'humour' – one can argue, on the contrary, that he is larger than life. In considering him as a comic figure, we return first to the definition of character by means of language, as we defined it in relation to Sam Weller, Jingle and Dick Swiveller. After the quiet currents of the narrative that chart the earliest days of David Copperfield's life, Dickens makes Mr Micawber, as David's London landlord, erupt on the scene in speeches of grandiloquent phraseology, said to be modelled on John Dickens's way of talking and writing. He offers to escort David to his house: ' "Under the impression," said Mr Micawber, "that your peregrinations in this metropolis have not as yet been extensive, and that you might have some difficulty in penetrating the arcana of the Modern Babylon in the direction of the City Road – in short," said Mr Micawber, in another burst of confidence, "that you might lose yourself – I shall be happy to call this evening, and instal you in the knowledge of the nearest way" ' (DC, ch. 11). His famous advice on leading a trouble-free life is also expressed in rhetorical fashion: 'Annual income twenty pounds, annual expenditure nineteen nineteen six, result happiness. Annual income twenty pounds, annual expenditure twenty pounds ought and six, result misery. The blossom is blighted, the leaf is withered, the God of day goes down upon the dreary scene, and – and in short you are for ever floored' (DC, ch. 12). There's a likeness here in this literary way of speaking with Dick Swiveller's extravagant expressions in *The Old Curiosity Shop* – and the conversational style is repeated in the utterances of Mrs Micawber, Micawber's affectionate and long-suffering wife. But Dickens makes Micawber an even more vital presence by displaying his optimism, indulgence in transient moments of self-pity and irrepressibility. On one occasion, David is shocked to receive a desperate letter from him about his financial plight: 'The die is cast – all is over.' But on his way to soothe him with 'a word of comfort' David meets the London coach with the Micawbers as passengers: 'Mr Micawber, the very picture of tranquil enjoyment, smiling at Mrs Micawber's conversation, eating walnuts out of a paper bag, with a bottle sticking out of his breast pocket' (DC, ch. 17). Nothing seems impossible with Mr Micawber and so we find convincing his unmasking of Uriah Heep's machinations and his eventual distinguished position as a District Magistrate in Port Middlebay, Australia. G.K. Chesterton, one of the most acute of Dickens's critics, professed himself at a loss for words in writing

about Micawber, a 'superman' that he could only admire with awe
(Chesterton, 1933, p. 139).

Evil-doers are present throughout Dickens's fiction, from Fagin
and his associates in *Oliver Twist* to John Jasper (we assume) in
The Mystery of Edwin Drood. His villains owe much to dramatic
convention in appearance, deed and gesture – this is not surprising
when we remember Dickens's love of the popular theatre from his
youthful days onwards. Freudian critics (like Edmund Wilson) have
detected possible suppressions and vicarious deeds and motives
rooted in Dickens's own emotions. Some of the villainous characters
are shadowy and threatening presences, like Monks in *Oliver Twist*
and Rudge (Barnaby's father) in *Barnaby Rudge*, who haunt their
victims. Monks, Oliver Twist's half-brother, who has stolen the boy's
inheritance and seeks to destroy him by some means or other, is seen
at first only as 'a dark figure' who emerges from shadow to whisper
in Fagin's ear. Nancy later gives an ominously detailed description of
him to Mr Brownlow: his 'lurking walk', his constantly looking over
his shoulder, his dark colouring, his 'withered and haggard face'. She
says that his 'lips are often discoloured and disfigured with the marks
of teeth; for he has desperate fits, and sometimes even bites his hands
and covers them with wounds' (OT, ch. 46). George Cruikshank,
who illustrated *Oliver Twist*, drew a frightening picture of Monks
and Fagin gazing silently through a window at Oliver Twist sleeping
in a chair in his little room in the Maylies' house: when Oliver
wakes, he sees next to Fagin ' white with rage, or fear, or both ... the
scowling features of the very man [Monks] who had accosted him at
the inn-yard' (OT, ch. 34).

Mr Rudge, the murderer who reappears many years after killing
Reuben Haredale and the gardener, who terrifies his wife and who
wanders here and there as a continually ominous figure, is at first
known only as 'the Stranger', but Dickens gives him a similar physi-
ognomy to Monks's, since he has 'the hard features of a man of
sixty or thereabouts, much weather-beaten and worn by time' and
a 'naturally harsh expression' and wears a dark handkerchief 'bound
tightly round his head' (BR, ch. 1). When his wife confronts him
in jail, Rudge's angry words are those of the melodramatic stage,
although Dickens toned down some of them in later editions:
' "Begone!" he cried. "Leave me! You plot, do you! You plot to get

speech with me, and let them know I am the man they say I am. A curse on you and on your boy." Faced with hanging, he falls into a 'paroxysm of wrath, and terror, and fear of death', smiting the stone floor of his prison cell with his 'ironed hands' (BR, ch. 73). (We recall the 'desperate fits' that afflict Monks.)

To a greater extent than Monks and Rudge, Daniel Quilp in *The Old Curiosity Shop* has a powerful physical dominance. Fearful and almost inhuman to look at, he is dwarf-like in stature but has a gigantic head and face. 'His black eyes were restless, sly, and cunning, his mouth and chin, bristly with the stubble of a coarse hard beard', made more grotesque by his mirthless 'ghastly smile'. His behaviour at the breakfast table is frightening: 'he ate hard eggs, shell and all, devoured gigantic prawns with the heads and tails on, chewed tobacco and water-cresses at the same time and with extraordinary greediness, drank boiling tea without winking, [and] bit his fork and spoon till they bent again' (OCS, ch. 5). Like Monks and Rudge, he pursues his human prey, appearing here and there in the narrative, as he tries to track down Little Nell and her Grandfather. Unlike them, there is something appallingly comic about Quilp, although a further dimension is added to his character by his lusting after Little Nell (who is still only thirteen), asking the alarmed and trembling girl whether she would like to be a second Mrs Quilp after his wife dies: 'to be my wife, my little cherry-cheeked, red-lipped wife' (OCS, ch. 6). The threat posed so often by Hugh, the ostler at the Maypole Inn in *Barnaby Rudge*, is similarly darkened by his sexual approaches to the pretty and vulnerable Dolly Varden. The villainy of all four men is appropriately punished, as it would have been in a melodrama on the stage. Monks dies penniless in prison in the New World, Rudge and Hugh are hanged, and Quilp drowns in the Thames while fleeing from arrest.

James Carker in *Dombey and Son* and Uriah Heep in *David Copperfield* are more insidious villains. Each resents his subordination to his employer (Mr Dombey and Mr Wickfield, respectively) and contrives to bring him to destruction. Dickens makes clear from the beginning the evil nature of each man by emphasizing his physical features. Carker, who could be a character from the melodramatic stage, has 'two unbroken rows of glistening teeth, whose regularity and whiteness were quite distressing. It was impossible to escape the observation of them, for he showed them whenever he spoke; and bore so wide a smile upon his countenance (a smile, however, very rarely, indeed, extending beyond his mouth) that there was something in it like the snarl of a cat' (DS, ch. 13). We are reminded of Hamlet's words that 'one may smile, and smile, and be a villain.' Dickens returns time and time again to those 'glistening teeth' (a more remarkable sight in Victorian days than in our age of cosmetic dentistry) as Carker pursues his course of financially ruining Mr Dombey as well as attempting to seduce his wife. Dickens emphasizes Carker's wickedness by showing his spiteful treatment of his unfortunate elder brother, John, who works alongside him in a subordinate position, and by revealing his past seduction and rejection of Alice Marwood. Uriah Heep is immediately repulsive, so that the reader anticipates villainy. He is cadaverous with close-cropped red hair – a style as unusual in the mid-nineteenth century as Carker's perfect teeth. He has 'hardly any eyebrows, and no eyelashes, and eyes of a red-brown, so unsheltered and unshaded' (DC, ch. 15) that [David Copperfield] wonders how he went to sleep. He has perpetually damp palms and a habit of snakily twisting his body. He insists on calling himself 'a very umble person', a description that becomes a motif in Dickens's presentation of Uriah like his repetition of Carker's menacing smile. Dickens's insistent repetition of facial features and catchphrases has often been deplored as an irritating trademark of his.

Uriah's intrigues are similar to Carker's, since he gradually exerts his domination over Mr Wickfield, his employer, and aims (to David's disgust) to make Agnes Wickfield his wife. Mr Micawber, who becomes a life-enhancing force for good in *David Copperfield*, exposes Uriah Heep's frauds. Heep ends in circumstances that are amusing to Dickens's readers but are a miserable punishment for him: he is jailed for 'fraud, forgery, and conspiracy' and sentenced to transportation for life. Carker's fate is as melodramatic as his stagey demeanour: Edith Dombey haughtily spurns him and in fleeing from Mr Dombey soon afterwards he falls to his death under a railway train that 'cast his mutilated fragments in the air' – an accident that Dickens describes in a paragraph of the kind of heightened dramatic prose of which he was a master (DS, ch. 55).

Little Dorrit has the most varied geographical settings of all the novels: France (Marseilles and Calais), London, Switzerland and Italy (Rome and Venice), as well as connections with China (whence Arthur Clennam has returned) and a 'barbaric power', possibly Russia (where Doyce goes to develop his unspecified invention). Dickens is explicit about the multitude of characters whose paths cross and recross in this complex narrative that involves prisons and family secrets: 'And thus ever, by day and night, under the sun and under the stars, climbing the dusty hills and toiling along the weary plains; journeying by land and journeying by sea, coming and going so strangely, to meet and to act and react on one another, move all we restless travellers, through the pilgrimage of life' (LD, I, ch. 2).

Almost inevitably, the villain of the novel is a mysterious man of no settled name, nationality or place: Rigaud, sometimes calling himself Blandois and Lagnier, is an adventurer and criminal, whose father was Swiss, whose mother was French 'by blood, English by birth', and who was born in Belgium. He is imprisoned temporarily in Marseilles because he was accused of murdering his wife (wrongly accused, so he claims, but his guilt is widely believed); gets involved with the Gowans in Italy; discovers and threatens to reveal Mrs Clennam's deceits and past history. As with Carker's gleaming teeth and Uriah Heep's reiteration of his humbleness, Dickens seizes on a particular characteristic to mark out Rigaud on his widely dispersed appearances: when he laughed, ' a change took place in his face, that was more remarkable than prepossessing. His moustache went up under his nose, and his nose came down over his moustache, in a very sinister and cruel manner' (LD, I, ch. 1). We have seen Dickens's emphasis on the frightening smiles on the faces of Quilp and Carker. Not surprisingly, Rigaud's life ends as violently and melodramatically as Quilp's, Carker's and Krook's: he is crushed to death when Mrs Clennam's decrepit house physically and symboli-cally collapses: 'it was night for the second time when [the diggers] found a dirty heap of rubbish that had been the foreigner [Rigaud], before his head had been shivered to atoms, like so much glass, by the great beam that lay upon him, crushing him' (LD, II, ch. 31).

Two rogues distinguished by their brutality appear in Dickens's last two completed novels: *Great Expectations* and *Our Mutual Friend*. Dickens gives Dolge Orlick in *Great Expectations* a name that by its ugliness suggests his nature – although he (or rather Pip, the narrator) tells us that 'Dolge' was 'a clear impossibility'. Orlick, Joe Gargery's journeyman in the blacksmith's forge, is a 'broad-shouldered loose-limbed swarthy fellow of great strength, never in a hurry, and always slouching' (GE, ch. 15). His air of menace is reminiscent of the demeanour of Hugh the ostler in *Barnaby Rudge*. He hates Mrs Gargery and assaults her with a convict's leg-iron, permanently injuring her mentally and physically and so eventually causing her death. He confesses to this attack much later when he imprisons Pip in a deserted sluice house with the intention of killing him. In association with Compeyson, he unsuccessfully tries to get Magwitch arrested and sentenced to death. Dickens puzzlingly contrives no just deserts for Orlick but gives us instead a facetious account of his breaking into Uncle Pumblechook's house – Joe tells Pip that among other humiliations 'they stuffed his mouth full of flowering annuals to perwent his crying out' (GE, ch. 57) – and subsequent imprisonment in the county jail. Swinburne complained that only Dickens 'could have eluded condemnation for so gross an oversight as the escape from retribution of so important a criminal as the "double murderer and monster"' (Hyder, 1972, p. 234). Another controversial point that arises in discussions of Dickens's presentation of Orlick is that he is arguably an *alter ego* of Pip, representing the suppressed darker side of the hero's character.

As with Orlick, Dickens's naming of Rogue Riderhood (whose actual Christian name was Roger) in *Our Mutual Friend*, incontrovertibly stamps him as a villain. He is a perpetual menace to others, wrongly accusing Gaffer Hexam, his former partner, of causing the death of John Harmon in order to get a reward, and he seems immortal. He is apparently drowned when his boat is run down by a steamer on the Thames in a fog but he slowly recovers from unconsciousness: 'the low, bad, unimpressible face is coming up from the depths of the river, or what other depths, to the surface again' (OMF, III, ch. 3). Knowing that Bradley Headstone has tried to kill Eugene Wrayburn, he fishes out Headstone's discarded clothes from the river and in a magnificent scene of terrifyingly black comedy he enters Headstone's classroom: '"I ask your pardon, learned governor," said Riderhood, smearing his sleeve across his mouth as he laughed with a relish, "'tain't fair to the lambs [the schoolboys] I know. It wos a bit of fun of mine. But upon my soul I drawed this here bundle out of a river! It's a bargeman's suit of clothes. You see, it had been sunk by the man as wore it, and I got it up"' (OMF, IV, ch. 15). A scene like that, coming late in the novel, shows, by the way, that Dickens's dramatic powers and mastery of prose were undiminished, despite the conventional accusation that those creative gifts had diminished by this time.

Chapter Fifteen
Hard Times, Little Dorrit, A Tale of Two Cities

Hard Times (1854)

This novel is the shortest that Dickens wrote (due in part to its serialization in weekly instalments in *Household Words*) and is the only one with no London scenes. Mr Gradgrind, who is retiring from his occupation as a hardware merchant and is about to become the local MP, lives in the northern industrial town of Coketown (perhaps modelled on Preston). His utilitarian philosophy of life is based on fact and rationality, as expressed in his opening words in a schoolroom, 'Now, what I want is, Facts.' On the other hand, Sleary's 'horse-riding circus', which is visiting Coketown, represents Fancy in the entertainment it offers. Although Gradgrind disapproves of the circus, he agrees to take care of Sissy Jupe, the daughter of one of Sleary's performers, who has disappeared. Gradgrind arranges a marriage beween Louisa, one of his daughters, to the boastful, aggressive businessman, Bounderby. She resignedly agrees to the marriage in order to help the prospects of her scapegrace brother, Tom. Stephen Blackpool, a weaver in one of Bounderby's mills, is in love with Rachael, but is married to a drunken wife, whom he cannot divorce because of contemporary laws. He is ostracized by his trade union for refusing to join a strike and decides to leave Coketown. To add to his miseries, he is soon afterwards accused of robbing Bounderby's bank, a crime committed by Tom Gradgrind. Returning to clear his name, he falls into a disused mine and dies from his injuries. Louisa, who resists the advances of James Harthouse, a ne'er-do-well young gentleman from London, runs away from Bounderby and finds comfort with Sissy Jupe, who has become an established member of the Gradgrind household. Sissy, who is a beneficent and loving influence, persuades Harthouse to leave Coketown. Bounderby's false claims of triumphing over a poor upbringing are revealed, Tom is exposed as a thief and Mr Gradgrind (like Mr Dombey) comes to realize the primacy of the heart's affections. The main comic element in this mostly serious novel is provided by the personality and pretensions of Mrs Sparsit, Bounderby's housekeeper, who dwells on her aristocratic connections, who has secret aspirations to marry Bounderby and who mistakenly thinks that Louisa is implicated with Harthouse in a love affair.

Dickens dedicated *Hard Times* to Thomas Carlyle, who had long and eloquently attacked the 'machinery' of the age. John Ruskin, whose anti-materialism was broadly in line with that of Carlyle, wrote in an instalment of *Unto this Last* (August 1860) that the novel in his opinion was 'in several respects the greatest [Dickens had] written' (Wall, 1970, p. 160). Bernard Shaw was another admirer, asserting in an Introduction to the novel (1913) that 'the increase in strength and intensity is enormous' (Laurence and Quinn, 1985, p. 30). But most readers then and later thought little of it, as it lacked the colourful richness of his previous fiction and seemed overdidactic. F.R. Leavis's 'Analytic Note' on the novel in *Scrutiny* that was reprinted in *The Great Tradition* (1948) was influential in establishing the novel as a 'completely serious work of art' (Leavis, 1962, p. 249). It became a favourite set book on school and college syllabuses, helped by its comparative brevity. Gradgrind has joined those Dickens characters like Scrooge and Pecksniff whose names are synonymous with deplorable human qualities.

Little Dorrit (1855–57)

Little Dorrit is Amy Dorrit, a seventeen-year-old girl who was born in the Marshalsea Prison, where her father is still imprisoned for debt as the novel opens. She has a brother, Edward, and a sister, Fanny. Arthur Clennam, a forty-year-old bachelor, has returned to England after working in his father's business in China. He meets

Little Dorrit when she is working as a seamstress for Mrs Clennam, the woman he assumes is his mother. Pancks, the agent for Mr Casby, a landlord, discovers that Mr Dorrit is the heir to a fortune, with the result that he is released from prison. The Dorrit family travel in Europe but at a dinner in Rome, given by Mrs Merdle, the wife of a prominent banker, Mr Dorrit confusedly reveals his past as a prisoner, collapses, and dies soon afterwards. Arthur Clennam finds himself falling in love with Pet Meagles, the daughter of a retired middle-class businessman, but she marries the arrogant Henry Gowan. Clennam meets his childhood sweetheart, Flora, but is disillusioned to find her a fat, prolix woman, accompanied by a fierce companion, her late husband's aunt. Pancks persuades him to invest in Merdle's business, but the bank collapses, Merdle commits suicide, and Arthur is ruined and imprisoned in the Marshalsea. A complex series of secrets is revealed: Mrs Clennam is Arthur's stepmother and she suppressed the codicil of a will that left Little Dorrit a considerable sum of money. Her house collapses just before she herself collapses and dies. Arthur is released from prison and marries Little Dorrit. A sinister presence throughout is that of Blandois, also known as Rigaud, who unearths some of the vital secrets of the Clennam family.

Dickens had thought of calling the novel 'Nobody's Fault', since his intentions included the exposure of the frustrations and inefficiencies of bureaucracy (satirized in his descriptions of what he called the Circumlocution Office) and of financial corruption (personified in Mr Merdle). The Crimean War, which was taking place at the time of the serialization of the novel, had also revealed disastrous administrative shortcomings. The grim subject matter and the intricate plot made the novel less appealing to readers who hankered after the colourful improvisations of Dickens's early books. But just as F.R. Leavis's appreciation of *Hard Times* led to a revaluation of that book so Lionel Trilling's Introduction to the Oxford Illustrated Dickens edition was influential in establishing its reputation as a masterpiece of English fiction: 'one of the most profound of Dickens's novels and one of the most significant works of the nineteenth century.' Trilling's basic point was that it was 'about society in relation to the individual human will' (Trilling, 1953, pp. v–vi).

A Tale of Two Cities (1859)

Scott's *Waverley* (1814) and Dickens's *Barnaby Rudge* are both set in periods sixty years before the dates of publication. Dickens uses a similar interval (about seventy years) in *A Tale of Two Cities*, his second historical novel. The 'two cities' are London and Paris during the time of the French Revolution. Doctor Manette, who has been imprisoned in the Bastille for eighteen years, is brought back to England by Mr Lorry, who works in Tellson's Bank in London and by Lucie, Manette's eighteen-year-old daughter. He has been lodging with Monsieur and Madame Defarge, who keep a wineshop in Paris. Charles Darnay, who is a member of the aristocratic French family, the Evremondes, and who lives in England, is tried at the Old Bailey on a false charge of treason. He is acquitted when his likeness to Sydney Carton, a lawyer involved in the case, shows that proof of his identity is uncertain. He and Lucie marry, although it is clear that Carton is also devoted to her. When the Revolution breaks out and the Bastille is stormed, Defarge finds Doctor Manette's cell, where he has secreted an account of the Evremondes' evil actions – they had contrived his imprisonment to silence him. When Darnay travels to Paris in response to a plea from a former servant, he is arrested. Defarge produces Doctor Manette's statement that implicates Darnay as a member of the Evremonde family and Darnay is therefore sentenced to death. Carton drugs him in his prison cell, changes clothes with him, and is guillotined in his place. Other characters include the comic 'resurrection man', Jerry Cruncher, who proves that a spy named Cly faked his own death; Barsad, another spy, who is Miss Pross's brother. Miss Pross, Lucie's companion, fiercely resists Madame Defarge's attempts to seize Lucy and her baby daughter, leading to Madame Defarge's accidental death.

The novel has the most memorable beginning and ending of all of Dickens's novels. Dickens opens it with his evocation of the period ('It was the best of times, it was the worst of times') and ends it with Carton's words on his way to the guillotine ('It is a far, far better thing that I do, than I have ever done ...'). Throughout he emphasizes action rather than character, a technique that was 'a deliberate and planned departure' from his usual method (Forster, IX, 2). In his Preface to the first edition (1859), Dickens wrote that it was one of his hopes 'to add something to the popular and picturesque means of understanding that terrible time, though no one can hope to add anything to the philosophy of Mr Carlyle's wonderful book [*The French Revolution*]'. The novel was appropriately dedicated to Carlyle, who had lent many books to Dickens as source material. *A Tale of Two Cities* has never ranked highly in critical esteem but its exciting narrative and moving climax have made it enduringly popular.

Chapter Sixteen
Theatre and Entertainment

During Dickens's lifetime, plays, theatres and playwrights proliferated, though hardly any dramatic works of lasting worth were produced. In London, many of the older theatres were rebuilt between 1800 and 1850 at the same time as many new ones were built or converted. The two principal theatres were those that had been long established in Covent Garden and Drury Lane, and other leading centres of dramatic entertainment included the Theatre Royal in the Haymarket, Sadler's Wells and the Lyceum. William Charles Macready, one of Dickens's closest friends, was one of the most influential actors and managers in the first half of the nineteenth century. Henry Irving, the charismatic Victorian actor, played a number of Dickens roles but did not decisively make his mark until shortly after Dickens's death when his performance in *The Bells* (1871–72) electrified everyone who saw him – he also became a vivacious Jingle and got to know the Dickens family well. Douglas Jerrold, Dion Boucicault, Tom Taylor, Mark Lemon, James Robinson Planché, John Madison Morton and Sheridan Knowles – some of whom were acquaintances of Dickens – were among the popular dramatists. Literally thousands of plays were staged: melodramas, farces, burlesques, comedies and tragedies, sometimes combined in multiple programmes – when David Copperfield went to Covent Garden, *Julius Caesar* and a pantomime were on the same bill, as we shall see. Adaptations of Dickens's novels were frequently dramatized, occasionally before their serialization was complete. Equestrian shows (like Mr Sleary's circus in *Hard Times*) were put on at Astley's Royal Amphitheatre in the Westminster Bridge Road. London had not the monopoly of dramatic activity, though Dickens knew its theatre world best of all in his early days – almost all provincial towns in Britain had their theatres. Travelling actors, singly and in troupes (like Jingle in *Pickwick Papers* and Vincent

Crummles's group in *Nicholas Nickleby*), entertained audiences, urban and rural, far and wide. Street entertainment was colourful and noisy, featuring musicians, conjurors and Punch and Judy men, such as we meet in *The Old Curiosity Shop*.

Dickens thought it vital that everyone should have opportunities for recreation and was happy to see that one means of relaxation for the poor was going to popular dramatic entertainments. In 'The Amusements of the People', a two-part paper he wrote in *Household Words* (30 March and 30 April 1850), he declared that there is 'a range of imagination in most of us, which no amount of steam-engines will satisfy; and which The-great-exhibition-of-works-of-industry-of-all-nations itself [i.e., the Great Exhibition planned for 1851] will probably leave unappeased'. He added that 'the lower we go, the more natural it is that the best-relished provision for this should be found in dramatic entertainments', and went on to describe his visit 'to see an attractive Melo-Drama called *May Morning, or the The Mystery of 1715, and the Murder'*, which was delightedly viewed by a packed audience of working-class men, women and children, together with some 'young pickpockets' of his acquaintance. He voices his belief in such needful amusement in the utterances of Miss Monflathers in *The Old Curiosity Shop* and Mr Sleary in *Hard Times*, which will be quoted later.

Dickens, like Thackeray his fellow novelist, had a love for the theatre that lasted all his life. He always remembered the first plays he saw when he was a little boy living in Chatham. In 'A Christmas Tree', memories of them come back to him: 'Yet again, I find myself before that vast green curtain. Yet again, the music plays, amidst a buzz of voices, and that fragrant smell of orange-peel and oil.' He recalled in 'Dullborough Town' (i.e., Chatham) that 'Richard III [in Shakespeare's play], in a very uncomfortable cloak, first appeared to me [at this theatre], and made my heart leap with terror by backing up against the stage-box in which I was posted, while struggling for life against the virtuous Richmond.' Pantomime was a particular source of joy, with its 'ten thousand million delights', including clowns, harlequins, pantaloons and columbines, as he recalled in his introduction to his edition of the *Memoirs* of Grimaldi (1838). As a young man in London, he frequented theatres, circuses, musical shows, fairs and pleasure gardens.

The excitement he felt is apparent in the response of David Copperfield, his fictional counterpart, to a performance of Shakespeare's *Julius Caesar* and 'the new pantomime' at the Covent Garden Theatre:

> the mingled reality and mystery of the whole show, the influence upon me of the poetry, the lights, the music, the company, the smooth stupendous changes of glittering and brilliant scenery, were so dazzling, and opened up such illimitable regions of delight, that when I came out into the rainy street, at twelve o'clock at night, I felt as if I had come from the clouds, where I had been leading a romantic life for ages, to a bawling, splashing, link-lighted, umbrella-struggling, hackney-coach-jostling, patten-clinking, muddy, miserable world. (DC, ch. 19)

Dickens even thought at one time, just before his career as a writer so sensationally took off, of becoming a professional actor but because of illness he was unable to keep an appointment for an audition in front of Charles Kemble, the celebrated actor, and Bartley, a stage manager. As well as visiting plays and other shows, Dickens was often involved in writing and adapting dramatic entertainments and in acting, directing and managing them. Out of the many productions he organized, two of the most successful were performances of Ben Jonson's *Every Man in his Humour*, with himself in the role of Captain Bobadil, and Shakespeare's *The Merry Wives of Windsor*, in which he was Mr Justice Shallow. He played the leading part of Richard Wardour in *The Frozen Deep* (1857), written by his friend and collaborator, Wilkie Collins, and this led to his meeting Ellen Ternan, who with her mother and sister took part as professional actresses in the performance in Manchester. From 1858 onwards, Dickens became obsessively involved in performing his solo programmes of highly acclaimed public readings from his novels and stories in Britain, Canada and the USA.

Dickens's novels are theatrical in many respects: sensational revelations and confrontations (like Mr Micawber's exposure of Uriah Heep in *David Copperfield*), high-flown rhetoric in passionate speeches (as in the climactic meeting between Edith Dombey and Carker in *Dombey and Son*) and exaggeration in characterization are often – but not invariably – present. John Ruskin, writing in *Unto this Last* (1860) about *Hard Times*, summed up Dickens's technique with typical directness and perception, warning us not to 'lose the use of Dickens's wit and insight, because he chooses to speak in a circle of stage fire' (Wall, 1970, p. 160). Robert E. Garis's *The Dickens Theatre* explored Dickens's showmanship as a vital and fundamental element in his fiction: 'Dickens is a performing artist, displaying his verbal skills in familiar modes and in a theatre created by the insistent self-delighting rhetoric of his voice (Garis, 1965, p. 63). As well as stage techniques, entertainment – perhaps we can even say 'show business' – is present in his fiction in in his depictions of characters like Mr Jingle and Vincent Crummles (mentioned above), in his descriptions of amateur performances and visits to theatres and circuses, and in his non-fictional accounts of places where the populace is enjoying itself.

Sketches by Boz at the very beginning of his career shows Dickens's fascination with London entertainments and his intimate knowledge of them. Among its 'Scenes' are the tea-gardens visited by 'Sunday-pleasurers' in 'London Recreations,' 'Astley's' (the equestrian theatre mentioned above), 'Greenwich Fair,' 'Private Theatres' (each of which 'constitutes the centre of a little stage-struck neighbourhood'), and 'Vauxhall Gardens by Day'. These 'scenes', apart from 'Astley's', are further animated by George Cruikshank's illustrations. In one of the 'Characters' in *Sketches by Boz*, 'The Misplaced Attachment of Mr John Dounce', Dounce and his friends sometimes go on a 'half-price visit to Drury Lane or Covent Garden, to see two acts of a five-act play, and a new farce, perhaps, or a ballet'. In another, 'Making a Night of It', Smithers and Potter 'go at half price to the slips at the City Theatre', where Potter's noisy heckling and mockery lead to their being 'shot with astonishing swiftness into the road'. Such high-spirited behaviour from members of the audience was not uncommon in the 1830s, well before the age of mid-Victorian respectability had set in. One of the youthful Dickens's 'Sketches of Young Gentlemen' is 'The Theatrical Gentleman', whom he views with satirical affection. The young gentleman (perhaps like young men Dickens knew or perhaps like Dickens himself) affects an intimate knowledge of his subject, shown in his use of pet names for London theatrical establishments: 'Thus Covent Garden is the garden, Drury Lane the lane, the Victoria the vic, and the Olympic the pic.' He refers to actors and actresses in familiar terms and 'has a great knowledge of the private proceedings of actresses'.

Of the places of entertainment Dickens describes in *Sketches by Boz*, Astley's Royal Amphitheatre seems to have remained most fondly in his memory. Spectacular equestrian shows were performed on its large stage – the Battle of Alma fought in the Crimean War on 20 September 1854 was re-enacted there with 400 extras on 23 October. In his piece in *Sketches by Boz* (written some twenty years before that performance), Dickens seems to participate in the enjoyment of the audience, especially the children in family parties. He returns to Astley's twice in his novels. His liveliest evocation of its pleasures is in *The Old Curiosity Shop*, when Kit Nubbles and his family go there: 'little Jacob applauded till his hands were sore, Kit cried "ankor" at the end of everything, the three-act piece included, and Barbara's mother beat her umbrella on the floor, in her ecstasies, until it was nearly worn down to the gingham' (OCS, ch. 39). In *Bleak House*, Mr George, a former soldier and the proprietor of a shooting gallery, reads a playbill on Waterloo Bridge and accordingly decides to go to Astley's nearby: 'he is much delighted with the horses and the feats of strength; looks at the weapons with a critical eye; disapproves of the combats, as giving evidence of unskilful swordsmanship; but is touched home by the sentiments' (BH, ch. 21).

The three novels that are most fully concerned with popular entertainment are *Nicholas Nickleby*, *The Old Curiosity Shop* and *Hard Times*. In the first of these, Dickens presents us with the troupe of travelling actors in Portsmouth (Dickens's birthplace) under the management of Vincent Crummles, whose depiction as a comic figure has already been described. The chapters devoted to them are written with such enthusiastic detail about all aspects of their life and work that the reader might assume that Dickens himself had had first-hand experience of them (although he hadn't). Of all the Crummles family, the most remarkable is one of Mr Crummles's daughters, the Infant Phenomenon, supposedly only ten years old but with a suspiciously aged countenance: 'she had been kept up late every night, and put upon an unlimited allowance of gin-and-water from infancy, to prevent her growing tall' (NN, ch. 23). Dickens also introduces us to many sharply delineated actors and actresses in the company, flirtatious, quarrelsome and pretentious. He regales us with their costumes, the melodramatic plots of the plays, the decor of the theatre and the professional jargon. Nicholas Nickleby, who has decided to call himself Johnson, is recruited by Mr Crummles as a playwright and actor. When he expresses doubts about his ability to write a play, Mr Crummles solves the problem with his usual cheerful practice of using whatever is at hand by giving him a roll of paper from a table-drawer: 'Just turn that [a French script] into English, and put your name on the title-page' (NN, ch. 23). He plans to bring out the piece, he tells Nicholas, on Miss Snevellicci's 'bespeak night', when her friends and patrons will subscribe for the performance after some preliminary persuasion. Nicholas plays a part as a young lover – when he 'came on for his crack scene with Mrs Crummles, what a clapping of hands there was!' (NN, ch. 24). Smike (unbelievably) plays alongside Nicholas in a Shakespearean role: 'only let him be tolerably well up in the Apothecary in *Romeo and Juliet* [Crummles says emphatically] with the slightest possible dab of red on the tip of his nose, and he'd be certain of three rounds the moment he put his head out of the practicable door in the front grooves O.P.' (NN, ch. 22). In the middle of these provincial episodes Dickens moves the action of the novel to London, where in a fashionable theatre Mrs Nickleby and Mrs Wititterly foolishly (but amusingly) chat about Shakespeare and where Kate Nickleby is apprehensive about the advances of the rakish Sir Mulberry Hawk. Dickens reintroduces Mr Crummles later in the novel when Nicholas attends the farewell supper for him and his family on the eve of their departure for America.

After the 'facts' that are the keyword in the instruction given in Mr Gradgrind's school by Mr M'Choakumchild in *Hard Times*, 'fancy' is embodied in Mr Sleary's horse-riding show that is visiting Coketown and that has put up its tents near the school. Dickens's message is explicit in Mr Sleary's final words to Mr Gradgrind, spoken with his habitual lisp: 'Don't be croth to uth poor vagabondth. People muth be amuthed. They can't be alwayth a learning..., they an't made for it' (HT, III, ch. 8). As with Dickens's other 'symbols', like fog, prisons and London, 'fancy' is something realized in concrete forms – in the performers, their idiosyncrasies, their circus acts and their names. Sissy Jupe, whose loving influence overcomes the coldness that distorts the motivation of several characters in the novel, is the daughter of the so-called Signor Jupe, one of Mr Sleary's performers (who has mysteriously disappeared). Dickens shows the same delight in the world of popular entertainment as he showed in *Nicholas Nickleby* – indeed some of the characters and scenes are virtually interchangeable. Again, we have a large and varied cast, who insinuate themselves into the room where Mr Gradgrind and Mr Bounderby are waiting, beginning with 'two or three handsome young women … with their two or three husbands, and their two or three mothers, and their eight or nine little children, who did the fairy business when required'. Two of the performers are 'Mr E.W.B. Childers, so justly celebrated for his daring vaulting act as the Wild Huntsman of the North American Prairies, in which popular performace, a diminutive boy with an old face … assisted as his infant son', and Mr Sleary's daughter, Josephine, 'a pretty fair-haired girl of eighteen, who had been tied on a horse at two years old, and had made a will at twelve, which she always carried about her, expressive of her dying desire to be drawn to the grave by the two piebald ponies' (HT, I, ch. 6). At the end of *Hard Times*, Tom, fleeing from probable arrest, hides in the circus, disguised as a black servant. Mr Sleary explains the scene to Louisa Gradgrind and Sissy Jupe. ' "That'th Jack the Giant Killer – piethe of comic infant bithnith," said Sleary. "There'th a property-houthe, you thee, for Jack to hide in; there'th my Clown with a thauthepan-lid and a thpit, for Jack'th thervant; there'th little Jack himthelf in a thplendid thoot of armour; there'th two comic black thervanth twithe ath big ath the houthe, to thtand by it and to bring it in and clear it; and the Giant (a very ecthpenthive bathket one), he an't on yet" ' (HT, III, ch. 7).

The Old Curiosity Shop has two major theatrical characters in Dick Swiveller, with his habit of quoting popular songs often sung on the stage, and in Quilp, a frighteningly comic monster who could come from age-old melodrama or a freak show. As Little Nell and her Grandfather go on their wandering journey away from London, they come across Codlin and Short, 'two exhibitors of the freaks of Punch', among the tombs in a country churchyard. They had placed the Punch puppet on a gravestone but the other 'persons of the Drama' were scattered either on the ground or in a box. Dickens's inventory of these 'persons' is as astonishingly informative as his summaries of the plots of the plays that Mr Crummles's troupe performed: 'the hero's wife and one child, the hobby-horse, the doctor, the foreign gentleman who not being familiar with the language is unable in the representation to express his ideas otherwise than by the utterance of the word "Shallaballah" three distinct times, the radical neighbour who will by no means admit that a tin bell is an organ, the executioner, and the devil, were all here' (OCS, ch. 16). Dickens adds a gentle touch by showing us Little Nell's repairing Judy's clothes with her needle and thread.

Other entertainers Nell and her Grandfather meet included stilt-walkers, dancing dogs, a giant, a limbless little lady and a man who does card tricks. At the race course, they see jugglers, mountebanks, gipsy fortune-tellers, ventriloquists and conjurors as well as Codlin and Short's Punch and Judy show – sights and sounds that often frighten Little Nell. They are later befriended by Mrs Jarley, the proprietor of a travelling waxwork show, whom Dickens possibly modelled on Madame Tussaud. Mrs Jarley kindly employs Little Nell as a guide to her exhibits – 'divers sprightly effigies of celebrated characters, singly and in groups, clad in glittering dresses of various climes and times, and standing more or less unsteadily upon their legs, with their eyes very wide open, and their nostrils very much inflated, and the muscles of their legs and arms very strongly developed, and all their countenances expressing great surprise' (OCS, ch. 28). She went to great pains to conciliate visitors from young ladies' boarding schools by altering some of the effigies, so that Mr Pitt, for example, in a nightcap and bedgown became a likeness of Cowper, the poet, and Mary Queen of Scots, in 'male attire' became 'the complete image of Lord Byron'. Miss Monflathers, a headmistress, rebukes Little Nell for her working as a guide to the waxworks, uttering words that express a contrast that Dickens reiterated throughout his career in speeches, articles and fiction:

> 'Don't you feel how naughty it is of you,' resumed Miss Monflathers, 'to be a wax-work child, when you might have the proud consciousness of assisting, to the extent of your infant powers, the manufactures of your country; of improving your mind by the constant contemplation

of the steam-engine; and of earning a comfortable and independent subsistence of from two-and-ninepence to three shillings per week? Don't you know that the harder you are at work, the happier you are?' (OCS, ch. 31)

Dickens casts a satirical yet sympathetic eye on disastrous dramatic activities (which he probably preferred to successful ones) like those in 'Mrs Joseph Porter', in *Sketches by Boz*. The Gattleton family 'was infected with the mania for Private Theatricals' and turn their neat house upside down in preparation: 'the large dining-room, dismantled of its furniture and ornaments, presented a strange jumble of flats, flies, wings, lamps, bridges, clouds, thunder and lightning, festoons and flowers, daggers and foil, and various other messes in theatrical slang included under the comprehensive name of "properties".' That is a knowing list that the 'Theatrical Young Gentleman' would have been proud of. The Gattletons' production of *Othello* is a 'complete failure', as a triumphant Mrs Porter tells everybody, because of absurd costumes and fluffed lines: the 'audience went home at four o'clock in the morning, exhausted with laughter, suffering from severe headaches, and smelling terribly of brimstone and gunpowder.'

In *Great Expectations*, Pip and Herbert see a chaotic *Hamlet* with Mr Wopsle, under the stage name of Mr Waldengarver, in the title role. We feel that Dickens and the audience are united in their amusement: 'on the question whether "twas nobler in the mind to suffer", some roared yes, and some no, and some inclining to both opinions said "toss up for it"; and quite a Debating Society arose.' The audience admonish the gravedigger in a friendly way: 'Look out! Here's the undertaker a coming, to see how you're getting on with your work.' Pip and Herbert 'feel keenly' for Mr Waldengarver but nevertheless laugh 'from ear to ear' (GE, ch. 31).

Dickens was fascinated by the two worlds of theatre and reality. Mr Wopsle, the former parish clerk, has become Mr Waldengarver, the Gattletons' household is the setting for *Othello*, David Copperfield leaves inspiring fairy-tale scenes he has seen at Covent Garden for the crowded, wet London streets. It's a contrast that bewilders Little Dorrit when she goes backstage to see her sister, Fanny, who is a dancer at a shabby theatre: there was 'a maze of dust, where a quantity of people were tumbling over one another, and where there was such a confusion of unaccountable shapes of beams, bulkheads, brick walls, ropes, and rollers, and such a mixing of gaslight and daylight, that they seemed to have got on the wrong side of the pattern of the universe' (LD, I, ch. 20). For Dickens, the stage props and stage magic were both to be cherished.

Chapter Seventeen
Dickens and Christmas

Dickens and Christmas go together. It was the season of the year for which he felt the deepest affection. On 9 June 1870, the day of Dickens's death, Theodore Watts-Duncan, the man of letters who later took Swinburne under his wing, heard a London barrow-girl exclaim, 'Dickens dead? Then will Father Christmas die too?' (Collins, 1993, p. 173). The story is hard to believe but there is no doubt that many people identified Dickens with Christmas – as indeed they still do. *A Christmas Carol* was his most popular book and one that countless people also knew from dramatized versions.

Dickens revelled in parties during the Christmas season. His daughter Mamie recalled that he 'always deserted work for the week ... He was the fun and life of those gatherings, the true Christmas spirit of sweetness and hospitality (Dickens, 1897, p. 37). On Twelfth Night (6 January) 1843 – Twelfth Night was still celebrated in Victorian times – he invited guests, including Leigh Hunt and Captain Marryat, to come and make merry at his eldest son's sixth birthday, where they would be entertained with a magic lantern and 'divers other engines' (Letters, III, pp. 419–20). Jane Welsh Carlyle, Thomas Carlyle's wife, went to a 'joyous' party in the Macready household in December 1843, revelling in Dickens's magic tricks ('the best conjuror I ever saw') and a wild 'universal country dance': 'Dickens took home Thackeray and Forster with him and his wife "to finish the night there" and a *royal* night they would have of it I fancy! – ending perhaps with a visit to the watch-house' (Bliss, 1950, pp. 144–5).

In one of his earliest pieces of writing, 'A Christmas Dinner' in *Sketches by Boz*, which in many ways anticipates his description of the Cratchits' celebrations in *A Christmas Carol*, Dickens begins with an outburst that tells us immediately what he feels – and always felt – about what he calls the merriest of the 365 days of the year: 'Christmas time! That man must be a misanthrope indeed, in whose breast something like a jovial feeling is not roused – in whose mind pleasant associations are not awakened – by the recurrence of Christmas.' He goes on to rhapsodize about glasses filled with punch, a blazing fire, presents, the turkey, plum pudding and mistletoe. (This list was written in the 1830s, before Prince Albert's introduction into England of the Christmas tree in 1841, the sending of the first Christmas cards in the 1850s and the composition of many popular Victorian carols.) He makes clear above all that it's a joyful family gathering of all the generations, although there may be memories of one little vacant seat – Tiny Tim from *A Christmas Carol* immediately comes to mind as the prime example of such a melancholy possibility. Dickens evokes the season again in a similar way in 1850 in 'A Christmas Tree' after looking at 'a merry company of children assembled around that pretty German toy, a Christmas Tree.' He excitedly remembers toys, story books (including his favourite *Arabian Nights*), toy theatres and the waits, the Nativity and incidents from the life of Jesus, coming home from school for the Christmas holidays (again we think of *A Christmas Carol*, with its picture of Scrooge as a schoolboy) and ghosts. His sad remembrances of people who have departed this life find comfort in the Christian message, which Dickens seldom makes explicit in his writings: 'I see the raiser of the dead girl, and the Widow's Son; and God is good!'

A comparable rhapsodic evocation of the joys of Christmas introduces the Pickwickians' visit to Dingley Dell, the home of the Wardles: 'it was the season of hospitality, merriment, and open-heartedness.' Once more Dickens associates the season with family reunions: 'How many families, whose members have been dispersed and scattered far and wide, in the restless struggles of life, are then reunited, and meet once again in that happy state of companionship and mutual good-will, which is a source of such pure and unalloyed delight' (PP, ch. 28). The fact that a sentiment like this sounds platitudinous today is partly due to the image of Christmas that Dickens has popularized. Having said that, we can still note the possibility that this benevolent outlook on the season was not completely his innovation. Some commentators have suggested that there is a precedent in Washington Irving's *The Sketch Book of Geoffrey*

Crayon, Gent. (1819–20), written in England and first published in America. Dickens had long known and admired Irving's writings and later counted him among his friends. In five chapters, Irving, in the persona of Geoffrey Crayon. expresses his delight in the English Christmas, with its 'tone of solemn and sacred feeling that blends with our conviviality', and describes the family gathering and the feasting, dancing and jollification at Bracebridge Hall, as well as the church service on Christmas morning (Irving, 1912, p. 223). But despite any basic likenesses, Dickens's 'good-humoured' chapters (to use his own adjective) in the *Pickwick Papers* are more vivacious and entertaining than Irving's in their varied and distinctive personages (the Wardles and their relations, the Pickwickians, Sam Weller, Bob Sawyer, Benjamin Allen, the fat boy and 'eight or ten young ladies'), in their succession of events (the seasonal celebrations as well as the wedding at Dingley Dell of Isabella Wardle and Mr Trundle) and in their evocation of indoor and outdoor seasonal enjoyments (playing cards, dancing, eating, drinking from the wassail bowl, singing and skating). Dickens's prose is alive and responsive to every mood of joy and excitement. Here are Mr Pickwick and others dancing: 'hands across – down the middle to the very end of the room, and half-way up the chimney, back again to the door – poussette everywhere – loud stamp on the ground – ready for the next couple – off again – all the figure over once more – another stamp to beat out the time – next couple, and the next, and the next again – never was such going!' (PP, ch. 28). Here is Mr Pickwick on the ice, memorably illustrated by Phiz (whose 'Christmas Eve at Mr Wardle's' is equally lively): 'The sport was at its height, the sliding was at the quickest, the laughter was at the loudest, when a sharp smart crack was heard. There was a quick rush towards the bank, a wild scream from the ladies, and a shout from Mr Tupman. A large mass of ice disappeared; the water bubbled up over it; Mr Pickwick's hat, gloves, and handkerchief were floating on the surface; and this was all of Mr Pickwick that anybody could see [until he eventually emerges]' (PP, ch. 30). In the middle of the congenial narrative ('bless our editorial heart, what a long chapter we have been betrayed into!' as Dickens exclaims) Dickens interpolates 'The Story of the Goblins who Stole a Sexton', told by Mr Wardle at his aged mother's prompting as he fills out 'the wassail with no stinted hand'. It hardly needs saying that the telling of ghost stories was – and is – a traditional entertainment on Christmas Eve. In this tale, which in its plot and message is another anticipation of *A Christmas Carol*, Gabriel Grub, the sexton, a 'morose and lonely man', has a dream on Christmas Eve in which he is tormented by goblins. As a result he is ashamed of his churlish behaviour, wanders abroad for ten years, and eventually returns as a repentant man.

A Christmas Carol: A Ghost Story of Christmas, the most famous of Dickens's Christmas writings, was published in 1843 in an elegant small volume with illustrations by John Leech: four coloured lithographs and four woodcuts. Its structure of five so-called Staves (with their musical connotation) has the simplicity and effectiveness of a traditional story: a preliminary haunting by the ghost of Jacob Marley, Scrooge's dead business partner; three visits by the Spirits of Christmas Past, Present and Future with the visionary scenes they display to Scrooge; and finally the happy consequences of his conversion from miserliness to kindly generosity. Dickens presents the many scenes with the distinct colouring (whether bright or dingy) and spontaneity that are typical of his early writing. Outstanding among these are those in which little Fan (with the same Christian name as Dickens's own elder sister) comes to fetch her brother, the schoolboy Scrooge, home for Christmas from his boarding school; the Fezziwigs' ball; Christmas dinner at the Cratchits'; and the sordid pawnbroker's shop in Scrooge's supposed afterlife. Forster summed up the message of *A Christmas Carol* better than anyone else has done, interpreting it in the light of mid-Victorian moral attitudes:

> It told the selfish man to rid himself of selfishness; the just man to make himself generous; and the good-natured man to enlarge the sphere of his good nature. Its cheery voice of faith and hope, ringing from one end of the island to the other, carried pleasant warning alike to all, that if the duties of Christmas were wanting no good could come of its outward observances; that it must shine upon the cold hearth and warm it, and into the sorrowful heart and comfort it; that it must be kindness, benevolence, charity, mercy, and forbearance, or its plum pudding would turn to bile, and its roast beef be indigestible. (Forster, IV, 2)

Dickens had been spurred to write the book by what he and others had witnessed and read of the sufferings of the poor in the decade that was later called the 'hungry forties'. Thomas Carlyle had published *Past and Present* a few months earlier – a key text of the period that was a deeply felt exposure of the 'condition of England', as he called it. On 9 March 1843, the Second Report of the Children's Employment Commission on the terrible conditions of child labour in factories and mines was published. On 6 March 1843, Dickens wrote to Dr Southwood Smith, a Unitarian minister and sanitary reformer, who had sent him an early copy of the report, that he was 'perfectly stricken down' by it and that he proposed to write a pamphlet on the subject. He did not proceed with this plan, but on 10 March 1843, he again wrote to Southwood Smith that the latter 'will certainly feel that a Sledge hammer has come down with twenty times the force – twenty thousand times the force – I could exert by following out my first idea' (Letters, III, pp. 459, 461). It seems as if he was already thinking of putting the idea in fictional form. Dickens had also been deeply interested in the Government's Factory Bill of that year with its ultimately unsuccessful clauses on the provision of education for the poor. In a letter to Miss Burdett-Coutts on 16 September 1843, which will also be cited later, Dickens had warned that in the 'prodigious misery and ignorance of the swarming masses ... the seeds of [the country's] certain ruin are shown' (Letters, III, p. 562). When the Spirit of Christmas Present brings out from the folds of his robe 'two children: wretched, abject, frightful, hideous, miserable', Scrooge is appalled, and the Spirit explains that the boy is Ignorance and the girl is Want: 'Beware them both, and all of their degree, but most of all beware this boy, for on his brow I see that is written which is Doom, unless the writing be erased' (Stave 3). Leech's engraving of the confrontation between Scrooge and the two children is like many that he made for *Punch*, which had just begun publication as a reforming and satirical periodical and which often published cartoons exposing the sufferings of the poor.

Dickens's second Christmas book was *The Chimes: A Goblin Story of Some Bells that Rang an Old Year Out and a New Year In*, written in Italy and published in London in December 1844, with illustrations by no fewer than four prominent artists: Daniel Maclise,

John Leech, Richard Doyle and Clarkson Stanfield. Maclise drew a picture of Dickens reading *The Chimes* aloud on 3 December 1844 to a group of men including Frederick Dickens (his brother), Thomas Carlyle, Blanchard, Jerrold, Forster and Stanfield. The title was suggested by Shakespeare's 'We have heard the chimes at midnight' from *King Henry IV, Part 2* and by the sound of the bells Dickens heard in Genoa when he was staying there and beginning work on the book.

The Chimes has elements in common with *A Christmas Carol*: it is divided into four 'Quarters'; the central character has visions brought about by supernatural agents (on New Year's Eve) and as a result views life in a more understanding and benign way; and it has a social message. But the message is more explicit than it was in the previous Christmas book. Dickens explained his aims in a letter of 8 October to John Forster: 'I like more and more my notion of making, in this little book, a great blow for the poor. Something powerful, I think I can do, but I want to be tender too, and cheerful; as like the *Carol* in that respect as may be, and as unlike it as such a thing can be. The duration of the action will resemble it a little, but I trust to the novelty of the machinery to carry that off; and if my design be anything at all, it has a grip upon the very throat of the time' (Forster, IV, 5). On 16 November 1844, he wrote from Cremona in similar terms to Douglas Jerrold, inviting him to the reading of *The Chimes* mentioned above: 'I have tried to strike a blow upon that part of the brass countenance of Wicked Cant, where such a compliment is sorely needed at this time. And I think that the result of my training is at least the exhibition of a strong desire to make it a staggerer' (Letters, IV, p. 218). The main character in *The Chimes* is Trotty Veck, a pathetic but affectionately depicted ticket-porter who earns a few pence in carrying messages through the London streets. He is sure from what he has read and heard that the poor are undeserving: 'We seem to be dreadful things; we seem to give a deal of trouble; we are always being complained of and guarded against' (Chimes, 1st Quarter). Alderman Cute and Sir Joseph Bowley typify people in authority who either bully or patronize the poor. In a series of visions that Trotty has in a nearby belfry on New Year's Eve, the Goblin of the Great Bell and other phantoms show him scenes from the future involving members of his family and others in distress of different kinds. But the bells communicate a message of hope and happiness. Trotty wakes up to scenes of joy and celebration.

Dickens concludes with a deeply felt message to his readers (or his listeners) combined with reflections on the imaginary qualities of the art of narrative:

> Had Trotty dreamed? Or are his joys and sorrows, and the actions in them, but a dream; himself a dream; the teller of this tale a dreamer, waking but now? If it be so, O listener, dear to him in all his visions, try to bear in mind the stern realities from which these shadows come; and in your sphere – none is too wide, and none too limited for such an end – endeavour to correct, improve, and soften them. So may the New Year be a happy one to you, happy to many more whose happiness depends on you! So may each year be happier than the last, and not the meanest of our brethren or sisterhood debarred their rightful share, in what our Great Creator formed them to enjoy. (4th Quarter)

The Cricket on the Hearth: A Fairy Tale of Home (1845), illustrated by Leech, Doyle, Maclise, Stanfield and Edwin Landseer (whose engraving of Boxer, the dog, was especially popular), was welcomed by many readers, especially by those who had disliked Dickens's social message in *The Chimes*. Following the 'Staves' and 'Quarters' in which he had divided his first two Christmas books, Dickens divided this book into three 'Chirps'. He made the Cricket a 'little household god' whose chirp carries a message of cheer in this story concerned mostly with the fortunes of John Peerybingle, a carrier, and Dot, his wife. Marital misunderstandings are eventually cleared up, partly through the agency of the Cricket on the Hearth, who appears to John Peerybingle in 'Fairy Shape'. Among the other characters in the story, Tackleton, a businessman who is a 'domestic Ogre', becomes a reformed and sweetened man at the end of the story. *The Cricket on the Hearth* is thought of today as too cosy and sentimental but Dickens thought that its publication was highly successful. Thackeray, reviewing it in the *Morning Chronicle* on 24 December 1845, declared that 'it is a good *Christmas* book, illuminated with extra gas, crammed with extra bonbons, French plums and sweetnesses' (Thackeray, 1955, p. 88).

The fourth Christmas book, *The Battle of Life: A Love Story* (1846), illustrated by Doyle, Leech, Maclise and Stanfield, has personal reformation again as its theme, although this time not by supernatural means.. One of its principal characters, Dr Jeddler, refers caustically at the beginning to 'this preposterous and ridiculous business called Life' (Part the First). But when he eventually discovers that Marion, his younger daughter, had selflessly relinquished her lover to Grace, her elder sister, his outlook changes: 'It's a world full of hearts ... a serious world, with all its folly (Part the Third).

Dickens brings back the supernatural in *The Haunted Man and the Ghost's Bargain: A Fancy for Christmas* (1848), illustrated by John Tenniel (just beginning his long and distinguished career), Frank Stone, Stanfield and Leech. The 'haunted man' is Redlaw, a professor of chemistry, who (like Scrooge) is visited by a Spectre on Christmas Eve. The Spectre grants him forgetfulness but without memories Redlaw loses any feelings of compassion. But he finds redemption under the influence of Molly Swidger's loving nature. The therapeutic effects of memory, often associated with childhood experiences, were a fundamental theme in Dickens's writings for Christmas. Again we turn to Forster to elucidate the message: 'There may have been sorrow, but there was the kindness that assuaged it; there may have been wrong, but there was the charity that forgave it; and with both are connected inseparably so many thoughts that soften and exalt whatever else is in the sense of memory, that what is good and pleasurable in life would cease to continue so if these were forgotten' (Forster, VI, 4).

When Dickens collected these five Christmas books in a volume in the first cheap edition of his works (1852), he referred in his Preface to an important feature of his technique (which had been limited by constraints of space) and to the underlying benevolent feelings he sought to convey:

> The narrow space within which it was necessary to confine these Christmas Stories when they were originally published, rendered their construction a matter of some difficulty, and almost necessitated what is peculiar in their machinery. I never attempted great elaboration of detail in the working out of character within such limits, believing that

it could not succeed. My purpose was, in a whimsical kind of masque which the good humour of the season justified, to awaken some loving and forbearing thoughts, never out of season in a Christian land. I have the happiness of believing that I did not wholly miss it.

Dickens's annual Christmas books were eagerly awaited. In January 1849, a reviewer in *Macphail's Edinburgh Ecclesiastical Journal* of *The Haunted Man* wrote that 'a Christmas book from him is as regular as a Christmas goose', although he or she had a very low opinion of the book under review (Collins, 1971, p. 179). Dickens himself felt he had a responsibility to his public to produce kindly and uplifting Christmas reading. He was perturbed that his absorption in the composition of *Dombey and Son* in 1847 had prevented him from writing a Christmas book that year, since he wished not to leave 'any gap at Christmas firesides which [he] ought to fill', as he told Forster (Forster, VI, 1). But between 1850 (the year after *The Haunted Man*) and 1867 he pleased his public by writing short stories at the festive season. They were published in his weekly magazine, *Household Words*, from 1850 to 1859 and then in its successor, *All the Year Round*, from 1860 to 1867. Other writers also contributed to the Christmas numbers of the two magazines. Dickens often devised a frame into which the stories were set. They did not deal specifically with Christmas subjects but they were generally imbued with what Dickens called the 'Carol philosophy', conveying lessons – or at least feelings – of benevolence, tolerance and altruism.

An early example was the number in *Household Words* called 'The Seven Poor Travellers' (1854), in which six travellers, with Dickens as a narrator, tell tales round the fireside on Christmas Eve. Dickens's contribution included 'The Story of Richard Doubledick'. Its hero, whose surname echoes Dickens's name, is a soldier whose tale was topical in 1854, when the Crimean War was in progress. Other stories in this framework were written by George Augustus Sala, Adelaide Ann Procter, Wilkie Collins and Eliza Lynn. Dickens particularly valued Wilkie Collins's collaboration in this and other pieces, such as 'The Wreck of the Golden Mary' (1856).

Three innovative and remarkably successful Christmas stories were his contributions to 'Mrs Lirriper's Lodgings' (1863), 'Mrs

Lirriper's Legacy' (1864) and 'Doctor Marigold's Prescriptions' (1865). In the first two of these, Mrs Lirriper narrates episodes from her life as lodging-house keeper in a freewheeling, allusive style that has affinities to Dickens's technique in Mrs Nickleby's reminiscences and Flora Finching's confused memories in *Little Dorrit*. The style has sometimes been seen as a forerunner of the 'stream of consciousness' as practised in the early twentieth century by James Joyce and Virginia Woolf. Dickens plunges us straightaway into her breathless narrative:

> Whoever would begin to be worried with letting Lodgings that wasn't a lone woman with a living to get is a thing inconceivable to me my dear, excuse the familiarity but it comes natural to me in my own little room when wishing to open my mind to those I can trust and I should be truly thankful if they were all mankind but such is not so, for have but a Furnished bill in the window and your watch on the mantelpiece and farewell to it if you turn your back for but a second ...

The so-called Doctor Marigold, who is a cheapjack, tells his own story, with a poignant account of his adoption of a deaf-and-dumb girl, Sophy, and the course of her life. Dickens again writes a rapid and colloquial monologue, as in Marigold's sales pitch: 'Here's a pair of razors that'll shave you closer than the Board of Guardians, here's a flat-iron worth its weight in gold, here's a frying-pan artificially flavoured with essence of beefsteaks to that degree that you've only got for the rest of your lives to fry bread and dripping in it and there you are replete with animal food.'

Two more notable stories are 'Picking up Soot and Cinders', from 'Tom Tiddler's Ground' (1861), in which Mr Traveller confronts a Hermit, Mr Mopes (based on a real-life original, one James Lucas, whom Dickens had visited), who lives in squalor. Mr Traveller, as a persona of Dickens, upbraids him for his filthy condition and for isolating himself from the world: 'every man must be up and doing ... and all mankind are made dependent on one another.' 'The Signal-Man', one of the parts of 'Mugby Junction', is perhaps the best known today of the Christmas stories. It is an ingeniously contrived ghost story, an appropriate genre for Christmas, and reflects Dickens's love–hate relationship with railways.

The Christmas scenes in the *Pickwick Papers* and *A Christmas Carol* have achieved classic status in capturing the essence of the Dickensian Christmas in their conviviality and their message of goodwill to all men. In two of his last novels, Dickens ironically juxtaposes Christmas celebrations with feelings of apprehension and even with the possibilities of crime. In *Great Expectations*, Pip, already afraid that his theft from the pantry will be discovered, is bullied at the dinner table on Christmas Day by everyone except Joe: his sister, Uncle Pumblechook, the Hubbles and Mr Wopsle. 'They seemed to think the opportunity lost, if they failed to point the conversation at me, every now and then, and stick the point into me. I might have been an unfortunate little bull in a Spanish arena, I got so smartingly touched up by those moral goads' (GE, ch. 4). Pip's misery and apprehension, presented so economically and convincingly by Dickens, is brought to a dramatic end by the irruption into the room of the military party in search of the escaped convicts. It hardly needs saying that Pip's plight is enhanced by the distortion of the Christmas spirit by the adults tormenting him on a day when all should be joyful.

The contrast between festivity and something ominous is more obviously marked in *The Mystery of Edwin Drood*. Dickens sparsely evokes the 'seasonable tokens' in Closterham. 'Red berries shine here and there in the lattices of Minor Canon Corner; Mr and Mrs Tope are daintily sticking sprigs of holly into the carvings and sconces of the Cathedral stalls, as if they were sticking them into the coat-buttonholes of the Dean and Chapter. Lavish profusion is in the shops: particularly in the articles of currants, raisins, spices, candied peel, and moist sugar' (MED, ch. 14). Compare that clear, spare description with the exuberant prose of the scene when the Ghost of Christmas Present appears in *A Christmas Carol*! Jasper has arranged a meeting at his house on Christmas Eve between Neville Landless and Edwin Drood to try to bring about a reconciliation. Dickens, in key with the cryptic approach he shows in this novel, tells us nothing about the meeting itself. But it is preceded by references to Neville's purchase of boots and a heavy walking stick in preparation for a walking tour and by an encounter between Edwin Drood and an old woman who takes opium and who asks him for money. A violent storm, making chimneys topple in the street, breaks out that night. On Christmas Day, Jasper informs Mr Crisparkle that Edwin and Neville went down to the river to look at the storm and that he hasn't seen Edwin since. Neville, who started his planned walk early that morning, is apprehended on suspicion of involvement in Edwin's disappearance. The heading of the chapter when the meeting takes place is 'When Shall These Three Meet Again?', an ominous echo of the witches' chant in *Macbeth* – and the storm may also derive from that play. We remember, as Dickens often did, that the telling of spine-chilling stories is a Christmas custom.

From *Sketches by Boz* to *The Mystery of Edwin Drood* Dickens turns again and again to Christmas. Many people have faulted the sentimentality and insufficiently religious content of the benevolent teaching he sought to impart. Writing to Charles Eliot Norton on 19 June 1870, just after Dickens's death, John Ruskin found his loss 'very frightful', but asserted that he 'knew nothing of the nobler power of superstition.' 'His Christmas,' Ruskin wrote, 'meant mistletoe and pudding – neither resurrection from the dead, nor rising of new stars, nor teaching of wise men, nor shepherds' (Wall, 1970, p. 191). Dickens paid lip-service to the religious significance of Christmas but his message, as we have already seen in some of his authorial asides and addresses, was expressed in a wish (couched in typically practical terms) in 'What Christmas Is As We Grow Older', a paper he contributed to *Household Words* in 1851: 'Nearer and closer to our hearts be the Christmas spirit, which is the spirit of active usefulness, perseverance, cheerful discharge of duty, kindness, and forbearance!'

Chapter Eighteen
Dickens's Public Readings

Public lectures and readings were a valued feature of cultural life in Britain and America in the Victorian period. Carlyle's four series of lectures in 1837–40 (ending with the best known, 'Heroes and Hero-Worship'), Thackeray on 'The English Humorists' and 'The Four Georges', T.H. Huxley on scientific subjects, Charles Cowden Clarke's literary readings and Fanny Kemble's recitals of Shakespeare are just a few examples. Dickens, with his lifelong love of the stage, with his incomparable skills as a public speaker and with his urge to communicate with his readers, was an ideal performer of his own work. But Adolphus William Ward, one of Dickens's earliest biographers, disapproved of Dickens's hurrying from Genoa to London in order to read *The Chimes* to a group of his friends in December 1844.

> No sooner was the writing done, than the other half of his double artist-nature was seized with another craving. The rage which possesses authors to read their writings aloud to sympathizing ears, if such can be found, is a well-worn theme of satire; but in Dickens, the actor was almost as strong as the author, and he could not withstand the desire to interpret in person what he had written, and to watch its effect with his own eyes and ears. (Ward, 1882, p. 65)

Encouraged by the response of a small circle of friends in Switzerland when he read them the first part of *Dombey and Son*, Dickens wrote to Forster: 'I was thinking the other day that in these days of lecturings and readings, a great deal of money might possibly be made (if it were not *infra dig.*) by having one's having Readings of one's own books' (Forster, V, 5). Forster (like Ward) indeed thought it an undignified activity, as he made clear then and later.

Dickens's first public readings, of *A Christmas Carol* and *The Cricket on the Hearth*, were in Birmingham Town Hall on 27, 29 and 30 December 1853 in order to raise funds for an adult education institute in that city. After more readings for charity, he gave his first paid reading on 29 April 1858 at St Martin's Hall, London. This was a period when he welcomed extra money to help pay for the upkeep of Gad's Hill Place, which he had bought in March 1856, and when he sought energetic distraction from his marital troubles – he and his wife separated in May 1858 – and from the feelings aroused by his relationship with Ellen Ternan. From then until April 1869, Dickens gave public readings in England, Scotland, Wales, Ireland and America, only breaking from his arduous tours when he was engaged in writing his novels: *A Tale of Two Cities*, *Great Expectations* and *Our Mutual Friend*. Philip Collins has calculated that he gave about 472 public readings in all and that he earned from them about £45,000 (almost half the £93,000 that he left in his will) (Collins, 1975, pp. xxv, xxix). A typical programme would last about two hours, with a substantial piece followed by a lighter one. Prices of admission ranged from one shilling to seven shillings (for his Farewell Readings) To give an impression of the concentrated programmes he undertook, we note that in October 1859 he read in Ipswich, Norwich, Bury St Edmunds, Cambridge, Peterborough, Bradford, Nottingham, Oxford, Birmingham and Cheltenham. The physical and emotional strains were enormous – Dickens, who was already suffering from several ailments, often had to lie down to recover after each reading. There is little doubt that Dickens's unremitting exertions, despite warnings from his friends and doctors, hastened his early death.

Albert Smith and then – after Smith's death – George Dolby were the efficient managers of the reading tours, although Dickens as always was attentive to every particular. Dolby's *Charles Dickens as I Knew Him* (1885) is full of detail about the tours, especially the one in America between November 1867 and May 1868. His description of the reading platform indicates the care that he and Dickens took concerning the equipment and lighting:

At the back was a large screen consisting of a series of woodwork frames covered with canvas; this again was covered with a maroon-coloured cloth, tightly stretched. In the centre of the stage or platform was the table, on which was a slightly raised reading-desk. On the left hand of the reader, on either side of the table, were small projecting ledges – the one on the right for the water-bottle and glass, the other for his pocket-handkerchief and gloves. Further forward, and on each side of the stage, ran two uprights; these were gas barrels, secured with copper wire 'guys', securing the batten and reflector, and communicating above and below with another range of lights with reflectors, so that the reader's face and figure were fully and equally distinct to the vision of the audience, and no effects were marred either by too much light overhead or by super-effulgence below. (Dolby, 1885, pp. 13–14)

Dolby would carry out acoustic tests with Dickens before performances.

Of the twenty-one texts that Dickens prepared, the seven that he performed the most, according to Philip Collins, were 'The Trial from Pickwick', 'A Christmas Carol', 'Boots at the Holly-Tree Inn', 'Doctor Marigold', 'David Copperfield', 'Mr Bob Sawyer's Party', and 'Mrs Gamp'. The two surprises for modern readers in that list are the adaptations of the Christmas stories, 'Dr Marigold' and 'The Holly-Tree Inn', which are seldom read these days. Other popular readings were 'The Chimes', 'The Story of Little Dombey' and 'Nicholas Nickleby'. Dickens adapted the texts in order to gain the most striking dramatic effects, by cutting, rearranging and sometimes adding a few words and phrases. When he prepared 'The Story of Little Dombey', he concentrated on the key stages in Paul's life – his birth, the conversation with his father about money, his lodging with Mrs Pipchin, his schooldays at the Blimbers' establishment and his death, with its final image of the 'golden ripple on the wall'. As was his custom, he further modified the text for later readings. From the beginning he had cut out a number of characters, including Walter Gay, and by the end he had eliminated Miss Tox as well. He reduced the social content of the readings (for example, he omitted the terrible child figures of Ignorance and Want from *A Christmas Carol*), so that he could give full rein to comedy and pathos. He wrote down stage directions for his own guidance, but knew the texts so thoroughly (after as many as two hundred rehearsals) that he could dispense with them when facing the audience.

Dickens, revelling in his versatility, would modify the pitch, pace and accents of his voice and his facial expressions. Numerous accounts testify to the rapturous reception he received. George Dolby remembered how his reading of *A Christmas Carol* could move him and his listeners.

> The scenes in which appeared Tiny Tim (a special favourite with him) affected him and his audience alike, and it not unfrequently happened that he was interrupted by loud sobs from the female portion of his audience (and occasionally, too, from men) who, perhaps, had experienced the inexpressible grief of losing a child. So artistically was this reading arranged, and so rapid was the transition from grave to gay, that his hearers had scarcely time to dry their eyes after weeping before they were enjoying the fun of Scrooge's discovery of Christmas Day, and his conversation from his window with the boy in the court below. (Dolby, 1885, p. 26)

One of Dickens's outstanding readings was 'Sikes and Nancy', from *Oliver Twist*, performed with frightening force towards the end of his career. After the first public performance at the St James's Hall on 5 January 1869, the critic in *The Times* of 8 January acknowledged Dickens's power: 'Never, probably, through the mere force of reading was a vast concourse held so completely within the grasp of one man.' His portrayals of Fagin and Nancy were especially praised. Penelope Fitzgerald, the novelist and critic, writing in the *Observer* on 28 October 1990, remembered talking to an old lady whose mother had been present at a Dickens reading in Blackburn (probably on 19 April 1869): 'His face, she had been told, as he read, didn't simply turn red, or even dark, it was black. The audience sat in terror.' But Bernard Darwin, an urbane yet enthusiastic Dickensian, wrote in 1954 that he had 'always been brought up to believe that this was a piece of over-acting on Dickens's part since, when [Darwin's] father heard it at Cambridge, he hated Nancy's falsetto and thought her screams too horrible' (Williams, 1954, unnumbered page). Other dissentient voices were heard about other recitals. The youthful Henry James, who heard Dickens in America, referred in an entry in his Notebooks in March 1905 to 'the hard charmless readings (or *à peu près*)' (Matthiessen and Murdock, 1961, p. 319). In the vast number of opinions on the subject, none express indifference and the overwhelming majority are laudatory.

The potential in Dickens's writing for dramatic excitement and colourful characterization has tempted actors to give their own readings on the stage, radio and television. Bransby Williams was the best known of these in the first half of the twentieth century – his Scrooge, in a now outmoded histrionic style, was a favourite with audiences. Emlyn Williams, Miriam Margolyes (on Dickens's women characters), Philip Collins and Simon Callow are among the most memorable readers or recitalists of the past fifty years or so.

Chapter Nineteen
Dickens's Friends and Contemporaries

Dickens probably had a wider circle of friends and acquaintances than any of his fellow-writers. J.W.T. Ley, in *The Charles Dickens Circle* (1918), alludes to several hundred of these, even then overlooking some who had some connection with him. Dickens dedicated his works to relevant people he admired and he named some of his children after them. Most of them were men, as would be expected at that time, but they came from different generations in Britain and abroad. In alphabetical order, Hans Christian Andersen, Edward Bulwer-Lytton, Thomas Carlyle, Wilkie Collins, Ralph Waldo Emerson, John Forster, Elizabeth Gaskell, Leigh Hunt, Washington Irving, Douglas Jerrold, Walter Savage Landor, Mark Lemon, Henry Wadsworth Longfellow, Bulwer Lytton, Captain Frederick Marryat, Samuel Rogers and William Makepeace Thackeray were among those who came from the world of letters. Dickens's abiding fascination with the theatre was reflected in his friendship with William Charles Macready and the French actor Charles Albert Fechter. Among the artists Dickens knew were Hablot K. Browne (Phiz), George Cattermole, George Cruikshank, Augustus Egg, William Powell Frith, Edwin Landseer, John Leech, Daniel Maclise, Clarkson Stanfield, Frank Stone and his son, Marcus Stone – most of whom illustrated his books. Francis Jeffrey (Lord Jeffrey), judge and critic, and Sir Thomas Noon Talfourd were prominent in the legal profession. James T. Fields, his publisher in Boston, USA and his wife, Annie, were close friends of his. He worked closely with Miss Angela Burdett-Coutts in her philanthropic enterprises, including the establishment of Urania Cottage as a home for 'fallen women'. The Reverend Chauncey Hare Townshend was involved not only in religious matters but also in mesmerism (an interest of Dickens's) and collecting. Dickens's acquaintances in upper-class and fashionable circles included the sixth Duke of Devonshire (in whose London residence, Devonshire House, he put on performances of amateur drama), Lord John Russell, Count D'Orsay and Lady Blessington, but needless to say he could never be on intimate terms with them in an age when social divisions were strictly marked. Nevertheless, he dedicated *Dombey and Son* to the Marchioness of Normanby and *A Tale of Two Cities* to Lord John. Of these people, many of whom were congenial and festive company, a few had an impact on his writing. That impact was always secondary to the originality and vision that he always displayed. He was the Inimitable Boz, supremely confident in his invention and technique, but on some occasions he was indebted to them in various respects.

Dickens's closest and most influential friend was John Forster. Forster was called to the Bar in 1845 but long before that he had established himself as a leading figure in literary London. He wrote literary and dramatic criticism for a variety of periodicals; edited the *Examiner*, the *Daily News* and the *Foreign Quarterly Review*; was the biographer of Oliver Goldsmith (1848), Landor (1869) and Dickens (1872–74), among others; and wrote works on seventeenth-century English history. He met Dickens in late 1836 at the house of William Harrison Ainsworth, the popular historical and Newgate novelist. Forster said after that first encounter that 'I left him as much his friend, and as entirely in his confidence, as if I had known him for years', and that the bond between him and Dickens 'remained unweakened till death came' (Forster, II, 1). Dickens, unwilling in those early days to refuse any commissions that came his way, had got into a tangle with publishers – Chapman and Hall, Macrone and Bentley – but Forster skilfully sorted out his contractual difficulties. He continued as a negotiator with publishers for the rest of Dickens's life, although Dickens sometimes used the services of others and was himself actively involved as well, letting nobody get the better of him. Forster negotiated the legal terms of Dickens's separation from his wife and drew up Dickens's will.

But his importance for readers is his involvement with the texts of Dickens's fiction. Dickens entrusted Forster with proof-reading, alone or in collaboration with him, a vital editorial task when Dickens was abroad (as he was for much of the composition of *Dombey and Son*). Dickens usually heeded his suggestions about characterization, plot and language – deletion, punctuation and the toning down of rhetoric, among other things. Forster's suggestion lay behind one of the most emotional and notorious scenes in Dickens's early novels: the death of Little Nell in *The Old Curiosity Shop*.

> I was responsible [he wrote] for its tragic ending. He had not thought of killing her, when, about half-way through, I asked him to consider whether it did not necessarily belong even to his own conception, after taking so mere a child through such a tragedy of sorrow, to lift her also out of the common-place of happy endings, so that the gentle pure little figure and form should never change to the fancy. (Forster, II, 7)

Dickens was aware that his language and invention might go over the top in *Barnaby Rudge*, a novel of violent passions and action. 'Don't fail,' he wrote to Forster on 5 April 1841, 'to erase anything that seems to you too strong.' He rejected Forster's complaint that he had been too sympathetic to the 'madman' Lord George Gordon (the instigator of the Gordon Riots in London in 1780) but took his advice about modifying an unsound feature of his original plan. Forster expressed his satisfaction: 'I was more successful in the counsel I gave against a fancy he had at this part of the story [the description of the Riots] that he should introduce as actors in the Gordon Riots three splendid fellows who should order, lead, control, and be obeyed as natural guides of the crowd in that delirious time, and who should turn out, when all was over, to have broken out from Bedlam' (Forster, II, 9). At Forster's urging, Dickens changed his mind about Walter Gay's career in *Dombey and Son*. As he worked on the early stages of the novel, Dickens asked Forster what he thought about his intention 'to show [Walter] gradually and naturally trailing away, from that love of adventure and boyish light-heartedness, into negligence, idleness, dissipation, dishonesty and ruin.' This course of action would show 'in short, that common, every-day, miserable declension of which we know so much in our ordinary life; to exhibit something of the philosophy of it, in great temptations and an easy nature; and to show how the good turns into bad, by degrees.' Forster dissuaded Dickens from developing Walter's character in this pessimistic way: 'For reasons that need not be dwelt upon here [in the *Life of Dickens*], but in which Dickens ultimately acquiesced, Walter was reserved for a happier future; and the idea thrown out took modified shape, amid circumstances better suited to its excellent capabilities, in the striking character of Richard Carstone in the tale of *Bleak House*' (Forster, VI, 2).

Forster's thoughtful devotion to Dickens's art, present in these and other particular instances, permeates his biography, published in 1872–74, soon after Dickens's death. He revealed to an unsuspecting public the story of Dickens's days in Warren's Blacking Warehouse, quoting from an autobiographical fragment that Dickens had given him. He reproduced Dickens's will, with its bequest of £1000 to Ellen Ternan at the head of all the bequests and provisions. But he was silent in the body of the text about the relationship between her and Dickens and was reticent about Dickens's separation from his wife. Forster could say little – even if he wanted to – about such personal matters since so many of the people were still alive. Omissions of this kind, in accordance with Victorian standards of decorum, do not invalidate the worth of an indispensable, deeply felt biography that has the classic status of Boswell's *Life of Johnson*. Mrs Q.D. Leavis was forthright in her opinion: 'The fact is that Forster, whatever his sins of omission, suppression, or alteration of some letters or documents to give himself greater importance in relation to Dickens in the eyes of the world, does give the only convincing representation of Dickens as the creator of the novels for those capable of reading them with critical perception and disinterestedness' (Leavis and Leavis, 1972, p. 10)

Forster bequeathed an immense quantity of Dickens material to the Victoria and Albert Museum in London. The Forster Collection includes the manuscripts of all Dickens's novels from *The Old Curiosity Shop* to *A Tale of Two Cities* and of large portions of *Oliver Twist* and *The Mystery of Edwin Drood*. (The Reverend Chauncey Hare Townshend, mentioned above, gave the manuscript of *Great Expectations* to the Wisbech and Fenland Museum.) There are many other manuscripts, proofs, letters, papers and books in the Forster collection. Dickens was typically not blind to Forster's idiosyncrasies and used him as the model for the aggressively patriotic Mr Podsnap in *Our Mutual Friend*. Leigh Hunt and Walter Savage Landor were two other friends he satirized – as Mr Skimpole (much to Forster's disapproval) and Mr Boythorn in *Bleak House*.

Dickens told his son, Henry Fielding Dickens, rather to his surprise, that 'the man who had influenced him most was Thomas Carlyle.' Henry Dickens could understand this statement with reference to *A Tale of Two Cities*, which has the French Revolution at its centre, but gathered that 'what he most admired in Carlyle was his sincerity and truth' (Oddie, 1972, p. 3). Thomas and Jane Welsh Carlyle, husband and wife, were friends of Dickens from 1840 onwards. When they first met, Carlyle had just established his reputation as a social critic and historian with the publication of *The French Revolution* in 1837, shortly to be followed by another astonishing work, *Past and Present* (1843), a poetic yet fact-based evocation of the 'condition-of-England question', to use Carlyle's term. He exposed the injustices of the existing system of government, vehemently attacked Benthamism and rationalism and championed work and effort. He looked to some kind of authoritarianism as a solution to the nation's problems and urged the necessity of religious belief in the widest sense. His teaching made a stirring impression on many writers of the time, including 'social novelists' like Elizabeth Gaskell and Charles Kingsley. Carlyle had reservations about the worth of popular writers of fiction such as Dickens but he recognized the appeal of his vivacious personality, was present at Dickens's reading of *The Chimes* in John Forster's house on the eve of its publication, and towards the end of Dickens's life roared with laughter at Dickens's public reading of the trial from the *Pickwick Papers*. (We have already seen how Jane Welsh Carlyle saw Dickens as the life and soul of a party at Macready's house.) Writing to the Dickens family on 4 July 1870, soon after Dickens's death, Carlyle said that 'every new meeting [since the first in 1840] ripened [their acquaintance] into more and more clear discernment of his rare and great worth as a brother man, a most cordial, sincere, clear-sighted, quietly decisive, just and loving man; till at length he had grown to such recognition with me as I have rarely had for any man of my time' (Forster, XI, 3).

Dickens's agreement with some of Carlyle's ideas is clear in *Hard Times*, which is dedicated to him. Carlyle had presented his 'Signs of the Times' as early as 1829 in an essay with that title in the *Edinburgh Review*: 'Were we required to characterize this age of ours by any single epithet, we should be tempted to call it, not an Historical,

Devotional, Philosophical, or Moral Age, but, above all others, the Mechanical Age. It is the Age of Machinery, in every outward and inward sense of that word' (Carlyle, 1915, p. 226). Commercialism – or the 'Mammon-Gospel', as he called it – was predominant, a belief that he deplored in *Past and Present*, written in the 'Hungry Forties': 'We have profoundly forgotten everywhere that Cash-payment is not the sole relation of human beings' (Carlyle, 1919, p. 132). Inhumanity and the neglect of the labouring poor were results of this materialistic outlook. Dickens's agreement with Carlyle's analysis and sympathies are embodied in Gradgrind and Bounderby on the one hand and in Stephen Blackpool on the other, though he falls short of suggesting Carlyle's 'heroic', strong-man remedies for the 'muddle' that confuses Stephen.

Dickens owes a considerable debt to Carlyle in *A Tale of Two Cities*. When *The French Revolution* first appeared he carried a copy of it wherever he went and in later life he used to say, with obvious exaggeration, that he had read it five hundred times. He asked Carlyle for other relevant books when he began work on the novel. Carlyle sent him a large number from the London Library, which Carlyle had helped to found in 1850. Dickens wrote to thank him on 24 March 1859: 'I cannot tell you how much I thank you for your friendly trouble, or how specially interesting and valuable any help is to me that comes from you. I do not doubt that the books received from the London Library, and suggested by you, will give me all I want' (Letters, IX, p. 41). In his Preface to the first edition of the *A Tale of Two Cities*, Dickens paid tribute to Carlyle's *The French Revolution* above all: 'It has been one of my hopes to add something to the popular and picturesque means of understanding that terrible time, though no one can hope to add anything to the philosophy of Mr Carlyle's wonderful book.' The 'philosophy', broadly speaking, was that the French Revolution was an inevitable shattering of inequality, oppression and 'imposture' (to use Carlyle's word) and that this consequence was an omen everyone should heed. Dickens similarly saw the Revolution as a struggle against suppression of human rights and also issued a warning at the end of *A Tale of Two Cities*: 'Crush humanity out of shape once more, under similar hammers, and it will twist itself into the same tortured forms. Sow the same seed of rapacious licence and oppression over again, and it will surely yield the same fruit according to its kind' (ATTC, III, ch. 15) This is not to say that Carlyle's message led to Dickens's message, which he would surely have independently conveyed. The teachings of both men coincided. Many incidents and some phraseology from *A Tale of Two Cities* derive from *The French Revolution*, particularly in Chapters 21 and 22, which dramatically describe the fall of the Bastille and the vengeful killing of Foulon. Dickens could admire in Carlyle's writing the heightened imagery, the rhythm and picturesqueness that were features of his own prose.

Clarkson Stanfield, the artist, introduced Dickens to Captain Frederick Marryat on 27 January 1841. They took to each other immediately. When Forster named many of Dickens's friends in his *Life of Dickens*, he said that if Marryat had not died in 1848 his name 'would have stood first among those I have been recalling, as he was among the first in Dickens's liking' (Forster, VI, 6), After a distinguished naval career, Marryat, like a number of sea captains of the time, turned to writing novels, first for adults and then for children. The novels for adults are boisterous, picaresque narratives, often with a seafaring content, and are still worth reading for their lively characters, humour and adventurous happenings. Those for children are similar, though a little toned down. The best known of his twenty completed novels are *Mr Midshipman Easy* (1836) and *The Children of the New Forest* (1847). Like Dickens, Marryat was a convivial man who enjoyed social gatherings and the company of children. Forster wrote that 'there was no one who approached [Dickens] on these occasions, excepting only our attached friend Captain Marryat, who had a frantic delight in dancing, especially with children, of whom and whose enjoyments he was as fond as became so thoroughly good hearted a man to be' (Forster, VI, 6). Dickens seems to have liked Marryat's books – he had thirteen volumes of his novels in his library at Gad's Hill as well as his *Universal Code of Signals* (1837) and his *Diary in America* (1839). On 15 October 1842, he wrote to Marryat: 'Many thanks for your famous book [perhaps *Percival Keene*, just published]; over which I have been chuckling, and grinning, and clenching my fists, and becoming war-like, for three whole days last past' (Letters, III, pp. 342–3). Dickens promised to send him a copy of his new book,

American Notes, in return – a book Marryat would appreciate, since he had also written of his experiences in America.

Likenesses of incident and character exist between Marryat's novels and Dickens's but these are likely to be coincidences arising from similarities of outlook and technique. No one has established any proof of indebtedness or (to put it more bluntly) plagiarism. Marryat uses the pseudo-scientific phenomenon of spontaneous combustion in *Jacob Faithful* (1833–34). Jacob on board a Thames lighter sees his father burst out of the cabin and jump to his death in the river. When Jacob investigates, he finds in the cabin 'a black mass in the centre of the bed' where his mother had been lying and informs his readers that she 'perished from what is termed spontaneous combustion'. He has already told us that she was a heavy drinker, who was 'a most unwieldy, bloated mountain of flesh' (ch. 1). Marryat's account of the revolting incident is vividly detailed but lacks the power and symbolism of Dickens's description of Krook's death in *Bleak House*. George Henry Lewes, in a vigorous attack on Dickens's belief in this popular 'scientific' fallacy, published on 11 December 1852 in the *Leader*, suggested that he had picked up the idea from his reading, since people may remember that Marryat 'employed the same equivocal incident in *Jacob Faithful*' (Ashton, 1992, p. 63).

Marryat's *Joseph Rushbrook* (1840–41) has some things in common with *Oliver Twist*. Joseph, its central figure, is a poor, downtrodden boy. When he arrives in London and is looking for a bed for the night. a little girl takes him into a thieves' den like Fagin's. He sees twenty boys and girls in the room, in the centre of which were 'huddled together on the floor, round a tallow candle, eight or ten of the inmates, two of them playing with a filthy pack of cards, while the others looked over them' (ch. 6). Another pathetic figure in Marrayat's fiction is Smallbones, Vanslyperken's persecuted cabin boy, in *Snarleyyow* (1836–37), who has been seen as a prototype of Smike in *Nicholas Nickleby*. Marryat introduces this 'thin, shambling personage' as someone who 'looked like Famine's eldest son just arriving to years of discretion'. His shrunken-looking clothes are like those Smike wears. 'His long lanky legs were pulled so far through his trousers, that his bare feet, and half way up to his knees, were exposed to the chilling blast. The sleeves of his jacket were so short, that four inches of bone were bared to view' (ch. 1). Some have claimed that the speech mannerisms of Cophagus, an apothecary, in Marryat's *Japhet in Search of a Father* (1834–35) were copied by Dickens in *Pickwick Papers* when he created Mr Jingle two years later. At one point in the story, Cophagus is unclear about Japhet's parentage: 'father, um – can't tell – love – concealment – child born – Foundling Hospital – put out – and so on' (ch. 62). But a quotation like that is enough to show that Marryat has little or nothing of Dickens's mastery of anecdote that he displays in Jingle's extravagant conversation.

After working for over ten years as a contributor to periodicals, William Makepeace Thackeray achieved some recognition with the publication in book form of *Barry Lyndon* (1844) and became a celebrity when *Vanity Fair* appeared as a monthly serial (1847–48). His other major novels were *Pendennis* (1848–50), *Henry Esmond* (1852), *The Newcomes* (1853–55) and *The Virginians* (1857–59). Dickens was never on close terms with Thackeray, who was widely seen at the time as his closest rival, though they often met on social and formal occasions. They first met in 1836, when Thackeray, who had trained as an artist in Paris, unsuccessfully proposed himself as an illustrator for *Pickwick Papers* after the suicide of Robert Seymour (who was eventually replaced by Phiz). In a speech at the Royal Academy Dinner in May 1858, Thackeray recalled 'walking up to [Dickens's] chambers in Furnival's Inn with two or three drawings in my hand, which, strange to say, he did not find suitable' (Melville 1910, II, p. 115). Thackeray, who had been educated at Charterhouse, one of the great public schools, and had briefly been an undergraduate at Trinity College, Cambridge, was conscious of his gentlemanly status and accordingly tended to look down on Dickens. Remarks here and there in his letters hint at the vulgarity (as he saw it) of the Dickens family. Towards the end of his life, he and Dickens quarrelled over the so-called Garrick Club Affair. Thackeray had been offended by a satirical sketch written about him by a fellow-member of the Garrick, Edmund Yates, whom he managed to get expelled from the club. Dickens, another member of the Garrick, supported Yates in the dispute. But not long before Thackeray died he and Dickens became reconciled – and their daughters were good friends.

Thackeray recognized, with reservations, Dickens's powers as a novelist, shown especially in his humour and in his appeal to the tenderer emotions, praising, for example, *A Christmas Carol*, *Dombey and Son* and *David Copperfield*. His own style and technique were less theatrical and colourful than Dickens's. Each novelist had his own supporters and advocates, a partisanship that lasted into the twentieth century. One contemporary critic, David Masson, reviewing *Pendennis* and *David Copperfield* in the *North British Review* in May 1851 summed up their basic differences: 'Thackeray is essentially an artist of the real school ... Dickens, on the other hand, works more in the ideal' (Tillotson and Hawes, 1968, p. 116).

Noting the less ornate prose of *David Copperfield*, Thackeray wondered whether his own prose style had had an effect on Dickens's style in that particular novel. Writing to Mrs Brookfield on 4 May 1849 just after he had read the first number of *David Copperfield*, he expressed his admiration for it but thought that he was responsible for a welcome change in Dickens's way of writing:

Have you read Dickens? – O it is charming. Bravo Dickens. It has some of his very prettiest touches – those inimitable Dickens touches wh. make such a great man of him. And the reading of the book has done another author a great deal of good. In the first place it pleases the other Author to see that Dickens who has long left off alluding to his the OA's works has been copying the OA, and greatly simplifying his style and forgoing the use of fine words. By this the public will be the gainer and David Copperfield will be improved by taking a lesson from Vanity Fair. Secondly, it has put me upon my mettle (Ray, 1945, II, p. 531)

In a letter of 6 (?) May 1851 to David Masson, whose comparison between the two novelists has just been mentioned, Thackeray stated that he quarrelled with Dickens's art in many respects, since it did not represent 'Nature duly; for instance Micawber [in *David Copperfield*] appears to me an exaggeration of a man, as his name is of a name.' But he went on to say that his writing was 'charming' (the adjective he had used in the letter to Mrs Brookfield) and that he doubted whether 'any novel-writer has that quality, that wonderful sweetness & freshness wh. belongs to Dickens' (Ray, 1945, II, pp. 771–3)

Dickens contributed a sympathetic obituary, 'In Memoriam', to the *Cornhill Magazine* in February 1864, a few weeks after Thackeray's death. He recalled their first meeting in 1836, when Thackeray sought to become the illustrator of *Pickwick Papers*, and wrote other 'remembrances' of times together. Dickens admitted that they had had 'differences of opinion', particularly about Thackeray's attitude towards the profession of literature – a criticism that had been made by others, including John Forster: 'I thought [Dickens wrote] that he too much feigned a want of earnestness, and that he made a pretence of undervaluing his art, which was not good for the art that he held in trust' (Tillotson and Hawes, 1968, p. 321). Thackeray's presentation of the London literary world in *Pendennis* (especially in Chapter 14) had incensed some writers.

Dickens's friendship in the latter part of his career with Wilkie Collins was as important as his friendship with Forster. They met on 12 March 1851 at Forster's house because Dickens was looking for an actor to take part in his amateur production of Bulwer-Lytton's play, 'Not So Bad As We Seem'. Their association, which began on that day, included writing and performing amateur dramatics, journalism and literary collaboration. Dickens and Collins went on jaunts together in Britain, France and Italy and their links became even closer when Wilkie Collins's brother, Charles, an artist, married Kate, Dickens's younger daughter (although Dickens came to dislike his son-in-law). Dickens admired Collins's professionalism and commitment to his writing and found liberating his unconventional behaviour in social and sexual matters. Collins dedicated *Hide and Seek* (1854), his fourth novel, to Dickens, 'as a token of admiration and affection'. In November 1856, Dickens brought him on to the staff of his weekly magazine, *Household Words*. He considered Collins at that time as someone who had benefited from his advice, as he told W.H. Wills, his assistant editor, in a letter on 10 July 1856: 'He and I might do something in *Household Words* together … [we] have talked so much in the last 3 or 4 years about Fiction-Writing, and I see him so ready to catch at what I have tried to prove right, and to avoid what I thought wrong, and altogether to go at it in the spirit I have fired him with' (Letters, VIII, p, 159). Collins had already contributed a short story, 'A Terribly Strange Bed', to the magazine in 1852.

He collaborated with Dickens and other writers on a number of stories in the Christmas numbers of *Household Words* and its successor, *All the Year Round*. In the former he contributed to the following joint stories: 'The Seven Poor Travellers' (1854), 'The Holly Tree Inn' (1855), 'The Wreck of the Golden Mary' (1856), 'The Perils of Certain English Prisoners' (1857) and 'A House to Let' (1858). In the latter there were 'The Haunted House' (1859), 'A Message from the Sea' (1860), 'Tom Tiddler's Ground' (1861) and 'No Thoroughfare' (1867). Collins's two most famous novels were first serialized in *All the Year Round*: *The Woman in White* (November 1859–August 1860), which set off the vogue for 'sensation novels', and *The Moonstone* (January–August 1868), which in T.S. Eliot's opinion was 'the first, and greatest of English detective novels' (Eliot, 1951, p. 464). His other novels included *Basil* (1852), *No Name* (1862) and *Armadale* (1866).

Dickens and Collins's *The Lazy Tour of Two Idle Apprentices*, serialized in *Household Words* (3–31 October 1857) is a high-spirited account, with two interpolated stories, of a tour they made of the north of England. The two apprentices are Francis Goodchild (Dickens) and Thomas Idle (Collins). Dickens, unhappy in his married life, had just fallen in love with Ellen Ternan and readers today can see suggestions of his feelings here and there. One of Dickens's contributions to the *Lazy Tour*, usually called 'The Bride's Chamber', is eerie and disturbing, since it tells of a bride who is willed to death by her husband. Light is thrown in the book on the contrasted characters of Dickens and Collins, as in these words addressed by Idle (Collins) to Goodchild (Dickens):

> To me you are an absolutely terrible fellow. You do nothing like another man. Where another fellow would fall into a footbath of action or emotion, you fall into a mine. Where any other fellow would be a painted butterfly, you are a fiery dragon. Where another man would stake a sixpence, you stake your existence. If you were to go up in a balloon, you would make for Heaven, and if you were to dive into the depths of the earth, nothing short of the other place would content you. (ch. 4)

Mutual influences may exist in the work of Dickens and Collins. In his essay, 'Wilkie Collins and Dickens' (first published 1927),

T.S. Eliot said that '*Bleak House* is the novel in which Dickens most closely approaches Collins (and after *Bleak House*, *Little Dorrit* and parts of *Martin Chuzzlewit*).' Eliot went on to claim that it 'is perfectly reasonable to believe that the relations of the two men – of which Forster gives us only the barest and most unsatisfactory hints – affected profoundly the later work of each. We seem to find traces of it in *Little Dorrit* and *A Tale of Two Cities*' (Eliot, 1951, pp. 461, 466). A particular likeness in the last-named novel origi-nates in Collins's play, *The Frozen Deep*, which incorporates many of Dickens's suggestions and which has as its central character, Richard Wardour, a part that Dickens acted to great acclaim. Wardour performs a courageous act of self-sacrifice in rescuing his rival in love and so is a possible forerunner of Sydney Carton in *A Tale of Two Cities*. Collins's ingenious plotting and use of mystery that typify many of his novels may indeed have had some effect on Dickens's later fiction, although the attribution of any direct connec-tions needs to be treated with caution even when made by Eliot. But Dickens's high estimate of Collins's powers is clear. He wrote to W.H. Wills, his associate editor, that *The Moonstone* 'is prepared with extraordinary care, and has every chance of being a hit [in *All the Year Round*]. It is in many respects much better than any thing he has done' (Letters, XI, p. 385). Its ingenious plot may have given some ideas to Dickens, and on the other hand Collins's Sergeant Cuff, with his idiosyncrasies, may have been suggested by Inspector Bucket in *Bleak House*. Of all Dickens's novels, *The Mystery of Edwin Drood* has the kind of puzzles and possible hidden clues that Collins manipulated so skilfully.

Dickens met Edward Bulwer-Lytton (who became Lord Lytton) in the late 1830s probably as a result of an introduction by Forster, who had known Bulwer-Lytton for some time. Bulwer-Lytton was a prolific novelist, admired by many readers (who made him one of the best-selling authors of the age) but mocked by others (including Thackeray) who thought him pretentious. His novels were of many kinds *Pelham* (1828) was a so-called 'silver-fork novel' (though with a touch of satire) about life in high society, a type parodied by Dickens in *Nicholas Nickleby*, when he has Kate read aloud 'The Lady Flabella' to Mrs Wititterly (NN, ch. 28). *Eugene Aram* (1832) was a Newgate novel, showing a measure of sympathy with its protagonist, a murderer, and was therefore the kind of novel that Dickens was accused of writing in *Oliver Twist*, an accusation that annoyed him. One of the best-known works of Bulwer-Lytton's considerable output is *The Last Days of Pompeii* (1834), an historical novel that (unlike his other books) is still occasionally read today. Among his plays was 'Not So Bad as We Seem', which brought Dickens and Wilkie Collins together, and *Money* (1840), which is still sometimes staged. Bulwer-Lytton was also a prominent politician, becoming the Secretary of State for the Colonies in 1858–59. He was associated with Dickens in amateur theatrical performances and with the founding in 1851 of the Guild of Literature and Art, which aimed to provide pensions and welfare for authors and artists but which had comparatively little success. Dickens's admiration for Bulwer-Lytton is reflected in his naming his tenth child Edward Bulwer Lytton Dickens (nicknamed Plorn) in 1852. He commissioned him to write *A Strange Story* for *All the Year Round* in 1862.

As we have seen, Forster persuaded Dickens to bring about the death of Little Nell in *The Old Curiosity Shop* and to change the character and fortunes of Walter Gay in *Dombey and Son*. Bulwer-Lytton's intervention in the resolution of *Great Expectations* was more radical. Dickens's intention was to end the novel with the permanent separation of Pip and Estella: in his first version, they meet briefly by chance when she is driving a pony-carriage in Piccadilly and then go their separate ways. But Bulwer-Lytton objected to this negative conclusion and Dickens, aware of the preferences of the reading public, altered the ending accordingly.

You will be surprised to hear that I have changed the end of *Great Expectations* from and after Pip's return to Joe's, and finding his little likeness there [i.e., Joe and Biddy's son]. Bulwer, who has been, as I think you know, extraordinarily taken with the book, so strongly urged it upon me, after reading the proofs, and supported his view with such good reasons, that I resolved to make the change. You will have it when you come back to town. I have put in as pretty a little piece of writing as I could, and I have no doubt the story will be more acceptable through the alteration. (Forster, IX, 3).

Thomas Noon Talfourd, a barrister (and later judge) and Member of Parliament, was one of Dickens's most congenial friends from the beginning of his writing career. As well as his legal and parliamentary work, Talfourd was a poet, dramatic critic and the author of *Ion*, a tragedy (1835), in which Macready played a leading role. He had known Lamb, Wordsworth and Coleridge. With his wife and family, he held convivial gatherings at his house in Russell Square in London. Dickens, who was frequently troubled (angered, in fact) by questions of copyright in Britain and abroad, admired his success in introducing a Copyright Bill in Parliament in 1837, which received the Royal Assent on 1 July 1842, and took his advice on the matter on a number of occasions. He dedicated the *Pickwick Papers* to Talfourd, who was the vice-chairman at the celebratory dinner given by the publishers on the completion of the novel. Talfourd, like Forster and Bulwer-Lytton, got involved in the fate of Dickens's characters, pleading on behalf of Charley Bates and the Artful Dodger in *Oliver Twist*. It is widely assumed that Talfourd was the model for Thomas (Tommy) Traddles in *David Copperfield*, partly because the Christian names are the same. After his death, Dickens paid tribute to him in 'The Late Mr Justice Talfourd', published in *Household Words* on 25 March 1854: 'The hand that lays this poor flower on his grave, was a mere boy's when he first clasped it ... Each of its successive tasks through many intervening years has been cheered by his warmest interest, and the friendship then begun has ripened to maturity in the passage of time; but there was no more self-assertion or condescension in his winning goodness at first, than at last.'

Angela Burdett-Coutts, who first met Dickens in 1839, inherited vast wealth from the Coutts banking family, and was known as the richest woman in England. She was a remarkable hostess, who entertained everyone worth knowing at the time and who was on close terms with the Royal Family. Dickens dedicated *Martin Chuzzlewit* to her. Many of her philanthropic enterprises engaged Dickens's attention, who became deeply involved in their programmes and administration. His correspondence with her over these and other matters (including his own family problems) is extensive. On her behalf he investigated the newly established Field Lane Ragged School in Holborn, London, and detailed its shortcomings to her on 16 September 1843: 'I have very seldom seen, in all the strange dreadful things I have seen, in London and elsewhere, anything so shocking as the dire neglect of soul and body exhibited among these children' (Letters, III, p. 562). He urged her to send financial help, which she agreed to do, but in the end little alleviation was possible. He was actively concerned for many years in the running of Urania Cottage, a house they opened in November 1847 in Shepherd's Bush, London, for the rescue and accommodation of 'fallen women' – it housed thirteen inmates under two superintendants. Dickens typically emphasized the necessity of order, cleanliness and regular domestic duties and concerned himself with every conceivable practical detail in the running of the house. On a personal level, Miss Burdett-Coutts was one of Charles Dickens junior's godparents and paid for his fees at Eton. She used her influence to nominate Walter, Dickens's second son, for a cadetship in the East India Company's 26th Native Infantry. Dickens attempted to justify to her his separation from his wife but she took Catherine Dickens's part (even inviting her to share her home, though Mrs Dickens declined her offer) and tried unsuccessfully to bring about a reconciliation.

Chapter Twenty
Great Expectations, Our Mutual Friend, The Mystery of Edwin Drood

Great Expectations (1860–61)

Pip (whose full name is Philip Pirrip) tells his own story. He lives at a forge in the Kent marshes with his harsh sister, the wife of Joe Gargery, the village blacksmith. While he is looking at the gravestones of his five deceased infant brothers in a nearby churchyard, he is terrified by the sudden appearance of Magwitch, an escaped convict, who makes him bring food and a file. But he and Joe soon witness the recapture of Magwitch together with his hated fellow-convict, Compeyson. Pip's Uncle Pumblechook takes him to Satis House, where he has been summoned by Miss Havisham to amuse her by playing. Miss Havisham, a recluse who has never recovered from being jilted, has a ward, Estella, a beautiful young girl, whom she is training to break men's hearts in revenge. Pip immediately falls in love with Estella, who treats him with disdain as a coarse working-class boy. He is therefore delighted a few years later to learn from a London lawyer, Mr Jaggers, that he has 'great expectations' of wealth and that he is to go to London to become a gentleman. He assumes that Miss Havisham is responsible for this change in his fortunes. He meets the eccentric lawyer's clerk, Wemmick, and shares chambers with Herbert Pocket, who becomes a valued friend. Ashamed of his humble upbringing, he lives lavishly, overspending his allowance. To his distress, Estella rejects his attentions and eventually marries the dissolute Bentley Drummle. At the forge, Mrs Gargery dies after an attack from an unknown assailant. Pip's pretensions are shattered when Magwitch reappears from

Australia, where he had been transported, and tells Pip that he is his benefactor. Miss Havisham is burnt to death at Satis House despite Pip's attempts to save her. Orlick, Joe's journeyman, captures Pip, confesses that he was Mrs Gargery's attacker, and is about to kill him when Pip is rescued. Pip tries to manage Magwitch's escape, since he has left Australia illegally, but Compeyson foils the plan, although he is drowned in a fight with Magwitch. Magwitch is sentenced to be hanged but dies beforehand. It is revealed that he was Estella's father. Dickens first ended the novel with a chance meeting in London between Pip and Estella, who had remarried after Bentley Drummle's death, a meeting that made clear they would see each other no more. But he was persuaded by Edward Bulwer-Lytton to write another ending: Pip and the widowed Estella meet (again by chance) in the desolate grounds where Satis House once stood. His concluding words suggest a hopeful future: 'I saw no shadow of another parting from her.' The two endings have always been the subject of controversy, with many readers in agreement with John Forster's judgement that 'the first ending nevertheless seems to be more consistent with the drift, as well as natural working out, of the tale' (Forster, IX, 3). On the other hand, Q.D. Leavis says that the rewritten ending is 'demonstrably superior to the one first intended and ... perfectly completes the intention and meaning of the novel' (Leavis and Leavis (1972, p. 425). For a full account and discussion of the endings, readers should consult Edgar Rosenberg's Norton Critical edition of the novel (1999).

The novel, told in the first person and presenting the childhood and early manhood of its hero, can be compared to *David Copperfield*. To avoid unconscious repetition, Dickens re- read the latter book as he was beginning *Great Expectations* (and told Forster that he 'was affected by it to a degree you would hardly believe' (Forster, 1X, 3)). It is a novel of popular appeal as well as one admired by critics. The portrayal of the themes of true and false love and of worthy and unworthy aspirations is sensitively conveyed in Pip's narrative. In addition, Dickens presents unforgettable scenes and people (the convicts on the marshes, Miss Havisham in Satis House, the attempted escape on the Thames) along with his usual varieties of comic observation (the touching humour of Joe Gargery's speech and actions, the eccentricities of Wemmick and the absurdities of Wopsle). The novel also has an ingenious plot that is not just surprising in its revelations but that vitally affects and reforms the hero.

Our Mutual Friend (1864–65)

'Our mutual friend' is John Harmon, heir to a fortune made by his late father by dealing in 'dust' (i.e., refuse). By the terms of his father's will, he can inherit only if he marries Bella Wilfer, whom he has never seen, as he has been living in South Africa. Returning to England, he wishes to land incognito, falls overboard in a quarrel and is presumed drowned. Calling himself John Rokesmith, he becomes secretary to Mr Boffin, who was old Harmon's foreman and who has inherited the Harmon money because of John's presumed death. Mr and Mrs Boffin have adopted Bella Wilfer, with whom he genuinely falls in love. Bella, who is openly mercenary, rejects him. Boffin tests her character by pretending to become miserly and dismisses Rokesmith from his employment. Bella thereupon reforms, leaves the Boffins and marries Rokesmith, whose true identity remains unknown to her. Eventually Boffin confesses that his miserliness was a subterfuge and Rokesmith reveals that he is John Harmon. Alongside this narrative runs the story of Lizzie Hexam, the poor but beautiful daughter of Gaffer Hexam, a Thames boatman who gets his living by finding corpses in the river, including the supposed body of John Harmon. She has a brother, Charley, whose schoolmaster, Bradley Headstone, falls passionately in love with her. Eugene Wrayburn, an idle young gentleman, also loves her. Without confessing it, Lizzie loves him, despite the class difference that seems to make impossible any close association. In a fit of jealousy, Headstone attacks Wrayburn, who falls into the river with terrible injuries but is rescued by Lizzie. She and Eugene Wrayburn are married while he lies in bed apparently at the point of death, but he slowly recovers. Rogue Riderhood attempts to blackmail Headstone but in a fight they both fall in the river and drown. Dickens develops associated themes of class and money to accompany these two main plots: the social life of the upstarts, the Veneerings; the marriage of the Lammles, who discover that neither has money; Fledgeby's moneylending business; Mr Podsnap's insular boastfulness. The rascally Silas Wegg, in association with Mr Venus, a taxidermist, schemes to get hold of Boffin's money. At the bottom of the social scale are Betty Higden and Jenny Wren, the crippled dolls' dressmaker.

Opinions of *Our Mutual Friend* are sharply divided. The youthful Henry James in a review for *The Nation* on 21 December 1865 thought it 'the poorest of Mr Dickens's works (Wall, 1970, p. 164), but Jack Lindsay asserted that it was 'one of the greatest works of prose ever written' (Lindsay, 1950, p. 380). It is certainly valued more highly today than it used to be. The satire centred on the Veneerings, the portrayal of Mr Podsnap and the wedding of Lizzie and Eugene can rank with Dickens's greatest presentations of comedy and moving emotion. As with the controversies over the ending of *Great Expectations*, so questions arise about the development of the plot. Were Mr Boffin's change of heart and Eugene's recovery after-thoughts on Dickens's part? In his 'Postscript in Lieu of Preface' to the first edition, Dickens defended the main structure of the novel, the realistic will made by the elder Harmon and his depiction of Betty Higden's sufferings because of the Poor Law. He alluded to the 'terribly destructive accident' to the train he was travelling in on 9 June 1865 and to his climbing back into the carriage to rescue part of the manuscript of *Our Mutual Friend*. He didn't say, of course, that his travelling companions were Ellen Ternan and her mother.

The Mystery of Edwin Drood (1870)

In the first chapter, John Jasper, the choirmaster of the cathedral in Cloisterham, is struggling to regain consciousness in a London opium den. Back in Cloisterham, he welcomes his nephew and ward, Edwin Drood, who is engaged to be married to Rosa Budd, in accordance with their late parents' wishes. Neville and Helena Landless, twins from Ceylon, arrive. Neville quarrels with Edwin in the presence of Jasper, who pretends to reconcile them but who has drugged their wine. When Durdles, the stonemason, takes Jasper to explore the cathedral buildings at night, Jasper drugs his drink so that he can temporarily steal his keys. Edwin and Rosa agree to end their engagement. Neville prepares to go on a walking tour and buys a heavy walking stick. A violent storm breaks out on Christmas Eve and Edwin Drood disappears. Neville is suspected of his murder. Jasper collapses when told of Edwin and Rosa's broken engagement. Mr Crisparkle discovers Edwin's watch and shirt-pin in Cloisterham Weir. The mysterious Dick Datchery arrives in Cloisterham, evidently a person in disguise. When Jasper declares to Rosa that he loves her and that he will see that Neville is hanged for the murder, she flees to Mr Grewgious, her guardian in London, is offered accommodation by Lieutenant Tartar and, with Miss Twinkleton (her former school-mistress), finds lodgings with Mrs Billickin. Jasper revisits the opium den, is followed back to Cloisterham by Princess Puffer, the opium woman, who Datchery sees spying on Jasper.

The story breaks off at this point because of Dickens's sudden death. Forster asserted that Jasper was to be revealed as the murderer and that 'the originality [of the novel] was to consist in the review of the murderer's career by himself at the close' (Forster, XI, 2). Other contemporaries, including Charles Dickens junior, Kate Perugini (Dickens's younger daughter) and Luke Fildes (the illustrator of the novel), agreed with Forster's statement. But a huge and never-ending Edwin Drood industry has flourished since the publication of the incomplete novel with solutions and completions ranging from the rational to the far-fetched. Leon Garfield wrote a well-received version, published in 1980. Interest in the plot has overshadowed consideration of other elements, such as theme, characterization and prose style. Some critics, influenced by biography, have thought the novel is evidence of Dickens's fading powers. Edmund Wilson, however, in 'Dickens: the Two Scrooges' (in *The Wound and the Bow*), said that the 'remarkable opening pages' contain 'perhaps the most complex piece of writing from the psychological point of view to be found in the whole of Dickens' (Wilson, 1961, pp. 90–1). Cecil Day Lewis thought that its characters 'include some of the liveliest he invented' (Day Lewis, 1956, p. 16). In 1870, Longfellow, hearing of Dickens's death, hoped that he had been able to finish writing the novel, which was 'certainly one of [Dickens's] most beautiful works, if not the most beautiful of all' (Forster, XI, 2).

Chapter Twenty One
Adaptations and Versions of Dickens's Writings

Stage adaptations of Dickens's work began immediately he started writing. 'The Christening', a farce by J.B. Buckstone, loosely based on 'The Bloomsbury Christening', published in the *Monthly Magazine* in April 1834 (and later collected in the *Sketches by Boz*), was staged at the Adelphi Theatre, London, on 13 October the same year. Plays derived from the *Pickwick Papers* were staged in London and New York in 1837 before its serialization was finished. Dramatizations of Dickens's work in London and elsewhere, at home and abroad, continued throughout the rest of the nineteenth century, becoming less numerous after the new century began. H. Philip Bolton calculates that by 1900 'about 200 playwrights had cultivated a luxuriant secondary theatrical growth of more than 1,000 productions of "Dickens dramas"' (Bolton, 1987, p. 43). William Thomas Moncrieff (with 'Pickwick Papers', 1837, and 'Nicholas Nickleby', 1839) and Edward Stirling, with at least twelve titles between 1837 and 1848, were active in the early propagation of this 'growth'. Nineteenth-century playwrights with more familiar names also adapted Dickens's novels and short stories. Don Boucicault wrote 'Dot' (1859), derived from *The Cricket on the Hearth*, and 'Smike' (1859), derived from *Nicholas Nickleby*. Tom Taylor adapted *A Tale of Two Cities* (1860). Even W.S. Gilbert (using the synonym, F. Latour Tomline) entered the field, with a version of *Great Expectations* (1871). Charles Dickens junior dramatized solely or in collaboration *The Battle of Life* (1873), *The Mystery of Edwin Drood* (1880, not staged) and *The Old Curiosity Shop* (1884). John Palgrave Simpson's 'Lady Dedlock's Secret' (1874) and 'All for Her' (1875) – the latter written in collaboration with Herman C. Merivale – were suggested by *Bleak*

House and *A Tale of Two Cities* respectively. Adaptations sometimes focused on a particular character, as seen in the Boucicault and Simpson titles just cited. Dolly Varden from *Barnaby Rudge* was a favourite heroine, giving her name to five or six plays. One of Henry Irving's popular roles was that of Jingle in James Albery's 'Pickwick' (1871), which was later renamed 'Jingle'.

Dickens regarded dramatizations of his work with mixed feelings. He was not alone in resenting the fact that owing to the law on copyright at the time he had no right to any of the money made by the plays. He deplored some of the performances and the liberties taken with his stories, especially the practice of putting them on the stage before their serialization was completed and writing endings of the adaptor's own devising. On the other hand, the extra publicity he gained was welcome. Forster makes clear Dickens's ambivalence when telling us of his responses to performances of *Oliver Twist* and *Nicholas Nickleby* in 1838. Forster says that he 'threw off lightly' the offences caused to his art perpetrated by Edward Stirling in his dramatization of *Nicholas Nickleby*: 'though I was with him at a representation of his *Oliver Twist* the following month at the Surrey Theatre, when in the middle of the first scene he laid himself down upon the floor in a corner of the box and never rose from it until the drop-scene fell, he had been able to sit through *Nickleby*, and to see a merit in parts of the representation ... [including] the capital manner and speech of Fanny Squeers [and Mrs Keeley's performance as Smike]' (Forster, II, 4).

But Dickens vehemently attacked the work of Moncrieff and other adaptors through the words of Nicholas Nickleby, who is infuriated by the condescending words of a 'literary gentleman' at Mr Crummles's farewell gathering: 'you take the uncompleted books of living authors, fresh from their hands, wet from the press, cut, hack, and carve them to the powers and capacities of your actors, and the capability of your theatres, finish unfinished works, hastily and crudely vamp up ideas not yet worked out by their original projector.' Nicholas asks the gentleman to show him the 'distinction between such pilfering as this, and picking a man's pocket in the street' (NN, ch. 48). Moncrieff issued from the New Strand Theatre a lengthy and angry address 'To the Public' in response, regretting that 'Mr Dickens should have lost his temper, and descended to scurrility and abuse, where a temperate remonstrance alone was needed' (Fitzgerald, 1910, p. 124).

Dickens, as a playwright himself, saw theatrical potential in his work, as we see in his own dramatizations ('The Strange Gentleman', for example, was based on 'The Great Winglebury Duel') and in his public readings. On 15 October 1859, just before the first appearance of *A Tale of Two Cities* in book form, he sent proof copies to François Régnier of the Comédie Française, wondering whether it could be staged in France (Letters, IX, pp. 132–3). He abandoned the idea when he realized that a performance would be politically unacceptable in that country. Tom Taylor wrote a dramatization of the novel a few months later. This kept to the main narrative thread, though Miss Pross and the final procession to the guillotine were omitted. Dickens approved of Taylor's version and attended rehearsals. On the title page of the printed text, Taylor acknowledged his help as 'one who has in the kindest manner superintended the production of the Piece'. The play opened at the Lyceum on 30 January 1860, had a successful run and transferred to the Bowery Theatre, New York, in the following year.

The most famous of all Dickens stage adaptations, again based on *A Tale of Two Cities*, was also staged at the Lyceum, almost forty years after Taylor's version. This was 'The Only Way', which opened on 16 February 1899. John Martin-Harvey, who was making his name as an actor, and his wife saw the opportunity to give him a starring role as Sydney Carton. Freeman Wills and Frederick Langbridge wrote a script that was further modified by Martin-Harvey and others. It was a very free version of Dickens's story with two climaxes: Carton's making an impassioned speech at Darnay's trial and his journey to the guillotine. It was extraordinarily popular in Britain and America – Martin-Harvey calculated he had acted in 5000 performances over a period of about thirty years.

Another great actor-manager at the turn of the century, Sir Herbert Tree, starred in Louis N. Parker's 'David Copperfield' (first staged in New York), which opened at the Haymarket Theatre, London, on Christmas Eve, 1914, soon after the outbreak of the First World War. Displaying his versatility, he took the roles of both Daniel Peggotty and Mr Micawber (alongside Owen Nares as David Copperfield). Chapman and Hall published a commemorative reprint of the novel, with photographs of actors and scenes from the production. Thereafter Dickens became less popular on the stage, partly because of films and radio, though there were three major exceptions on the London stage later in the century. Lionel Bart's musical, 'Oliver!', was a huge success in 1960 when it opened at the New Theatre, and became even more of a hit in 1968 as a film directed by Carol Reed – Ron Moody's Fagin rivalled Alec Guinness's as a definitive personification. In 1963, 'Pickwick', another musical, was staged at the Saville Theatre, with Harry Secombe in the title role. The script was by Wolf Mankowitz and the music by Cyril Ornandel. The outstanding theatrical adaptation was the Royal Shakespeare Company's production of 'Nicholas Nickleby' that opened at the Aldwych Theatre on 6 June 1980. Closely following Dickens's text, this was written by David Edgar and directed by Trevor Nunn and John Caird. The performance, which involved about forty actors, some of whom played several parts, lasted for a total of four-and-a-half hours, divided into two plays. This was by far the fullest adaptation of a Dickens novel that had been staged, giving an overwhelming impression of this multitudinous work with its intense humour, pathos and excitement. In an enthusiastic review for *The Times*, Bernard Levin wrote that the production was 'a celebration of love and justice that [was] true to the spirit of Dickens's belief that those are the fulcrums on which the universe is moved' (Rubin, 1981, p. 179). A film of the production was shown at the opening of Channel Four television in November 1982.

Michael Pointer, in his *Charles Dickens on the Screen* (1996) lists about one hundred silent films that were made between 1897 and 1927. Graham Petrie, in the first of three articles on 'Silent Film of Adaptations of Dickens', published in the *Dickensian* in 2001, agrees with this figure and points out that each of the novels was filmed at least once during those twenty years. He notes that the 'most frequently filmed titles in the silent era were *A Christmas Carol, The Old Curiosity Shop, The Pickwick Papers*, and especially *Oliver Twist*, with *The Cricket on the Hearth* making a surprisingly strong showing – titles that reflect quite accurately the popular preferences of the early years of the last century' (Petrie, 2001, p. 7). The last-named title was filmed in 1909 by D.W. Griffith, who was an admirer of Dickens's work, seeing affinities between his technique and cinematic practice. (Grahame Smith has explored such connections in his *Dickens and the Dream of Cinema* (2003). Other directors who filmed Dickens in these early days of the cinema included Cecil Hepworth, Maurice Elvey and Herbert Wilcox (who brought 'The Only Way' to the screen in 1925, with Sir John Martin-Harvey re-creating his leading role as Sydney Carton). In 1922, Frank Lloyd directed 'Oliver Twist', with Jackie Coogan (the child star of Chaplin's 'The Kid') as Oliver and Lon Chaney as Fagin.

The first famous Dickensian 'talkie' (to use a term of the 1930s) was George Cukor's 'David Copperfield' (1935), in which Freddie Bartholomew (another Hollywood child star) was the young hero and W.C. Fields a still-remembered Micawber. In the post-war years, a remarkable group of films appeared in Britain. These can be seen as celebrations of Englishness (like the eye-opening Festival of Britain in 1951) and as affirmations of the strength of the British film industry (also shown in the elegant and witty Ealing Comedies of the period). It is belittling to think of them as simply escapist, but they gloriously offset the drab environment of a country recovering from the privations of war and displayed the genius of Dickens. This was the time, too, of Laurence Olivier's three great Shakespearean films: 'Henry V' (1944), 'Hamlet' (1948) and 'Richard III' (1957), which can be seen to have a similar motivation. Foremost among the Dickens films were the two David Lean 'classics': 'Great Expectations' (1946) and 'Oliver Twist' (1948), characterized by striking opening sequences, atmospheric settings (Satis House and the London streets, for example), and superb acting (Bernard Miles as Joe Gargery and Alec Guinness as Fagin, to name only two performances). Splendid casts featured in Cavalcanti's 'Nicholas Nickleby' (1947), Brian Desmond Hurst's 'Scrooge' (with Alastair Sim in the title role, 1951), Noel Langley's 'Pickwick Papers' (with Nigel Patrick as the definitive Jingle and Donald Wolfit as Serjeant Buzfuz, 1952) and Ralph Thomas's 'A Tale of Two Cities' (with Dirk Bogarde as the hero, 1958).

Of the numerous film adaptations of Dickens that followed over the next fifty years, two should be mentioned. Christine Edzard's six-hour version of *Little Dorrit* (1987) consisted of two films that looked at the story from two different viewpoints: 'Nobody's Fault' (a title Dickens had thought of giving his novel) and 'Little Dorrit's

Story'. Again, the cast was formidable: Alec Guinness as Mr Dorrit (forty years after his Herbert Pocket and Fagin), Derek Jacobi as Arthur Clennam and Cyril Cusack as Frederick Dorrit were unforgettable. Roland Polanski's 'Oliver Twist' came out in 2005. Ronald Harwood, its scriptwriter, pointed out the empathy that existed between the director and Oliver: 'Roman was in the Krakow Ghetto: this is about a little boy who survives' (Lebrecht, 2005, p. 33).

From its beginning in the 1920s radio has been a popular medium for adaptations of Dickens. Early broadcasters included Bransby Williams in his trademark monologues and V.C. Clinton-Baddeley in sonorous readings, including his own version of *Bleak House* in sixteen instalments between January and April 1930. Microphone serials, as Val Gielgud, the Head of BBC Drama termed them, became an established feature of radio broadcasting during the 1940s, when plays adapted from Dickens, Thackeray, Jane Austen, Trollope and Tolstoy, among others, were avidly listened to during the war. The first of the Dickens serials was 'Scenes from Pickwick', devised in twelve instalments by Philip Wade, which began in October 1939, with 'Christmas at Dingley Dell' broadcast on Christmas Eve. Other novels soon followed. Howard Agg and Mabel Constandouros's 'Bleak House', transmitted in the autumn of 1944, attracted a large audience and led to a run on bookshops for copies of the novel – a demand that was often disappointed in those wartime days of shortages. Since that time radio adaptations of all the novels (in many versions) and a good deal of the short fiction have been frequently broadcast, invariably in conscientious and well-acted productions. The many adaptors, over a period of sixty years, include Audrey Lucas (one of the first), Mollie Hardwick, R.D. Smith, John Keir Cross, Vincent Tilsley and Charles Lefeaux.

Specially composed incidental music and sophisticated sound effects have increasingly become part of radio drama, as in Radio 4 productions of *Barnaby Rudge* (1995), *Pickwick Papers* (1997), *Bleak House* (1998) and *Little Dorrit* (2001) – in the last of these, scenes were recorded in Georgian houses in Spitalfields and Soho. One tendency at the beginning of the twenty-first century has been to divide novels into fifteen-minute sections in imitation of the original serialization. In 2006, 'David Copperfield' was presented in twenty instalments over a period of four weeks.

Stephen Harrison's 'Bardell Against Pickwick' was the first lengthy Dickensian television adaptation in Britain, transmitted in July 1938. At Christmas in the same year came performances of *A Christmas Carol*, with Bransby Williams as Scrooge. Television broadcasting shut down during the Second World War. When programmes resumed, 'The Only Way' was shown in February 1948 and Bransby Williams appeared yet again as Scrooge in *A Christmas Carol* in December 1950. Among adaptations of Dickens in the 1950s and 1960s were Vincent Tilsley's 'David Copperfield' (1956 and 1966), Freda Lingstrom's 'Our Mutual Friend' (1958–59), and Constance Cox's 'Bleak House' (1959) and 'Oliver Twist' (1962). These were live performances, with some filmed episodes, and were made in black and white. Arthur Hopcraft's 'Hard Times', televised on Granada Television in 1977 (by which time colour television was well established), made a considerable impact, with its forceful script, high production values and a cast that included Patrick Allen as Mr Gradgrind and Timothy West as Bounderby. Hopcraft's 'Bleak House' (1985) – shot entirely on film – and his 'A Tale of Two Cities' (1989) – an Anglo-French production – were two more outstanding adaptations. Three more productions that preserved true Dickensian qualities (especially atmosphere and characterization) were David Lodge's 'Martin Chuzzlewit' (1984), with a cast including Paul Scofield and John Mills; Sandy Welch's 'Our Mutual Friend' (1998); and Andrew Davies's 'Bleak House' 2005). This 'Bleak House' was transmitted in fifteen 30-minute instalments, twice a week, thus copying the style of presentation of TV 'soaps', as some commentators noted. In the *Radio Times* of 22–28 October 2005, Nigel Stafford-Clark, the producer, explained this mode of serialization: 'The reason we came up with the twice-a-week idea was because the BBC asked us to see if we could find a way to refresh the period drama format' (Stafford-Clark, 2005, p. 14). John Sutherland introduced, in a lively and scholarly manner, each week's instalments in the *Radio Times* and wrote a guide to the novel, *Inside Bleak House* (2005), to accompany the serial. Alan Bleasdale's reworking of *Oliver Twist* (1999) was a controversial version (a 'second draft', as Bleasdale called it) with a newly written introductory section, based on Dickens's ending and opening out the clues he gives there to the origins of Oliver's family and the predicament he finds himself in.

Robert Lindsay gave an electrifying central performance as a non-Jewish Fagin.

The adaptations and versions, whatever the medium, show the infinite riches that Dickens has to offer. Whatever their quality, something Dickensian always shines through, so powerful are his imaginative powers.

Further Reading

Numerous editions of Dickens are in print, with introductions and explanatory notes. The *Clarendon Dickens*, which began in 1966 under the general editorship of John Butt and Kathleen Tillotson and which is still in progress, publishes scholarly texts of Dickens's fiction. His journalism has been collected in the four volumes of the *Dent Uniform Edition of Dickens's Journalism* (1994–2000), edited by Michael Slater and John Drew. K.J. Fielding collected 115 of his *Speeches* (1960; rev. edn., 1988) and Philip Collins his *Public Readings* (1975). His letters fill twelve volumes of the Pilgrim edition, edited by Madeline House, Graham Storey, Kathleen Tillotson and others (1965–2002). Newly discovered letters are periodically published in the *Dickensian*, the journal of the Dickens Fellowship. The extensive annotation to these letters is an indispensable source of information concerning Dickens's life and times.

John Forster brought out the first authoritative biography in three volumes in 1872–1874. The annotated editions by J.W.T. Ley (1928) and A.J. Hoppé (1966; revised, 1969) add useful supplementary material. Three other biographies, out of the many that have been published, are notable: Edgar Johnson's *Charles Dickens: His Tragedy and Triumph* (2 vols, 1952), Peter Ackroyd's *Dickens* (1990) and Michael Slater's article in the *Oxford Dictionary of National Biography* (2004). John Butt and Kathleen Tillotson examine Dickens's methods in *Dickens at Work* (1957; reprinted, 1963, 1968). Jane R. Cohen gives an account of *Charles Dickens and his Original Illustrators* (1980). Collections of criticism include George H. Ford and Lauriat Lane's *The Dickens Critics* (1966), Stephen Wall's *Charles Dickens* (1970) and Philip Collins's *Dickens: The Critical Heritage* (1971).

Comprehensive works of reference are George Newlin's *Everyone in Dickens* (1995), Paul Davis's *Penguin Dickens Companion* (1999) and the *Oxford Reader's Companion to Dickens*, edited by Paul Schlicke (1999). Philip Collins compiled the bibliography in the

New Cambridge Bibliography of English Literature, Volume 3 (1969), reprinted as a separate booklet by the Dickens Fellowship in 1970. Paul Schlicke compiled the bibliography in the *Cambridge Bibliography of English Literature*, Volume 4 (1999).

Full details of the books in this list of Further Reading can be found in the Bibliography that follows.

Bibliography

Books

Ackroyd, P. (1990), *Dickens*. London: Sinclair-Stevenson.

Ackroyd, P. (1991), *Introduction to Dickens*. London: Sinclair-Stevenson.

Ashton, R. (1992), *Versatile Victorian: Selected Writings of George Henry Lewes*. London: Bristol Classical Press.

Auden, W.H. (1963), 'Dingley Dell and the Fleet', *The Dyer's Hand*. New York: Random House.

Bagehot, W. (1911), *Literary Studies* (2 vols). Everyman's Library. London: J.M. Dent and Sons Ltd.

Bliss, T. (1950), *Jane Welsh Carlyle: A New Selection of her Letters*. London: Victor Gollancz Ltd.

Bolton, H.P. (1987), *Dickens Dramatized*. London: Mansell Publishing Ltd.

Brain, R. (1960), *Some Reflections on Genius and Other Essays*. London: Pitman Medical Publishing Co.

Butt, J. and Tillotson, K. (1968), *Dickens at Work*. University Paperbacks. London: Methuen and Co. Ltd.

Carlyle, T. (1915), *Scottish and Other Miscellanies*. Everyman's Library. London: J.M. Dent and Sons Ltd.

Carlyle, T. (1918), *Past and Present*, ed. A.M.D. Hughes. Oxford: Clarendon Press.

Chancellor, E.B. (1924), *The London of Charles Dickens*. London: Grant Richard Ltd.

Chesterton, G.K. (1933), *Criticisms and Appreciations of the Works of Charles Dickens*. London: J.M. Dent and Sons Ltd.

Cohen, J.R. (1980), *Charles Dickens and his Original Illustrators*. Columbus: Ohio State University Press.

Collins, P. (1963), *Dickens and Education*. London: Macmillan and Co. Ltd.

Collins, P. (1964), *Dickens and Crime*. 2nd edn). London: Macmillan and Co. Ltd.

Collins, P. (1970), *A Dickens Bibliography*. Reprinted from the *New Cambridge Bibliography of English Literature* (1969), ed. G. Watson. London: Dickens Fellowship.

Collins, P. (1971), *Dickens: The Critical Heritage*. London: Routledge and Kegan Paul.

Collins, P. (1975), *Charles Dickens: The Public Readings*. Oxford: Clarendon Press.

Collins, P. (1981), *Dickens: Interviews and Recollections* (2 vols). London: Macmillan Press Ltd.

Darwin, B. (1933), *Dickens*. London: Duckworth.

Davies, J.A. (1983), *John Forster: A Literary Life*. Leicester: Leicester University Press.

Davis, P. (1999), *The Penguin Dickens Companion*. Harmondsworth: Penguin Books.

Davis, P.B. (1990), *The Lives and Times of Ebenezer Scrooge*. New Haven: Yale University Press.

Day Lewis, C. (1956), 'Introduction' to Charles Dickens, *The Mystery of Edwin Drood*. London and Glasgow: Collins.

Dickens, C. (1980), *The Mystery of Edwin Drood*, concluded by Leon Garfield. London: André Deutsch.

Dickens, C. (1999), *Great Expectations*, ed. Edgar Rosenberg. Norton Critical Edition. New York and London: Norton.

Dickens, H.F. (1928), *Memories of My Father*. London: Victor Gollancz Ltd.

Dickens, M. [1897], *My Father as I Recall Him*. Westminster: Roxburghe Press.

Dolby, G. (1885), *Charles Dickens as I Knew Him*. London: T. Fisher Unwin.

Dyos, H.J. and Wolff, M. (1973), *The Victorian City: Images and Realities* (2 vols). London: Routledge and Kegan Paul.

Eliot, T.S. (1951), *Selected Essays*. London: Faber and Faber Ltd.

Fawcett, F.D. (1952), *Dickens the Dramatist: On Stage, Screen and Radio*. London: W.H. Allen.

Fielding, K. (1988), *The Speeches of Charles Dickens*. Hemel Hempstead: Harvester Wheatsheaf.

Fitzgerald, S.J.A. (1910), *Dickens and the Drama*. London: Chapman and Hall.

Ford, G.H. (1965), *Dickens and his Readers*. New York: W.W. Norton Inc.

Ford, G.H. and Lane, L. (1966), *The Dickens Critics*. Ithaca: Cornell University Press.

Forster, J. (1928), *The Life of Charles Dickens*, ed. J.W.T. Ley. London: Cecil Palmer.

Forster, J. (1969), *The Life of Charles Dickens*, ed. A.J. Hoppe, (2 vols). Rev. edn. Everyman's Library. London: Dent and New York: Dutton.

Garis, R. (1965). *The Dickens Theatre*. Oxford: Clarendon Press.

Hawes, D. (1998), *Who's Who in Dickens*. London and New York: Routledge.

Hollingshead, J. (1900), *According to My Lights*. London: Chatto and Windus.

House, H. (1960), *The Dickens World*. Oxford Paperbacks. London: Oxford University Press.

House, M., Storey, G., Tillotson, K. *et al.* (1965–2002), *The Letters of Charles Dickens* (12 vols). The British Academy and Pilgrim Edition. Oxford: Clarendon Press.

Hughes, J.L. (1914), *Dickens as an Educator*. New York and London: D. Appleton and Co.

Hyder, C.K. (1972), *Swinburne as Critic*. London and Boston: Routledge and Kegan Paul.

Irving, W. (1912), *The Sketch Book of Geoffrey Crayon, Gent*. World's Classics. London: Oxford University Press.

Jackson, T.A. (1937), *Charles Dickens: The Progress of a Radical*. London: Lawrence and Wishart.

Jerrold, W.B. (1872), *London: A Pilgrimage*, illustrated by Gustave Doré. Reissued with an introduction by Peter Ackroyd (2005). London: Anthem.

Johnson, E. (1952), *Charles Dickens: His Tragedy and Triumph* (2 vols). London: Hamish Hamilton.

Laurence, D.H. and Quinn, M. (1985), *Shaw on Dickens*. New York: Frederick Ungar Publishing Co.

Leavis, F.R. (1962), *The Great Tradition*. Harmondsworth: Penguin Books Ltd.

Leavis, F.R. and Leavis, Q.D. (1972), *Dickens the Novelist*. Harmondsworth: Penguin Books Ltd.

Ley, J.W.T. (1918), *The Charles Dickens Circle*. London: Chapman and Hall.

Lindsay, J. (1950), *Charles Dickens: A Biographical and Critical Study*. London: Andrew Dakers.

Matthiessen, F.O. and Murdock, K.B. (1961), *The Notebooks of Henry James*. Galaxy Book. New York: Oxford University Press.

Melville, L. (1910), *William Makepeace Thackeray* (2 vols). London: John Lane, The Bodley Head.

Newlin, G. (1995), *Everyone in Dickens* (3 vols). Westport, CT and London: Greenwood Press.

Nicoll, A. (1955), *A History of English Drama 1600–1900*, Vol. 4. Cambridge: Cambridge University Press.

Oddie, W. (1972), *Dickens and Carlyle: The Question of Influence*. London: The Centenary Press.

Page, N. (1988), *A Dickens Chronology*. London: Macmillan Press.

Pemberton, T.E. (1888), *Charles Dickens and the Stage*. London: George Redway.

Picard, L. (2005), *Victorian London: The Life of a City*. London: Weidenfeld and Nicolson.

Poe, E.A. (1927), *Poems and Essays*. Everyman's Library. London: Dent.

Pointer, M. (1996), *Charles Dickens on the Screen*. London: Scarecrow Press.

Porter, R. (1993), *Disease, Medicine and Society in England 1550–1860* (2nd edn). London: Macmillan.

Priestley, J.B. (1925), *The English Comic Characters*. London: John Lane, The Bodley Head.

Ray, G.N. (1945), *The Letters and Private Papers of William Makepeace Thackeray*. (4 vols). London: Oxford University Press.

Ray, G.N. (1955), *Thackeray: The Uses of Adversity, 1811–1846*. London: Oxford University Press.

Ray, G.N. (1958), *Thackeray: The Age of Wisdom, 1847–1863*. London: Oxford University Press.

Rubin, L. (1981), *The Nicholas Nickleby Story*. London: Heinemann.

Schlicke, P. (1985), *Dickens and Popular Entertainment*. London: Allen and Unwin.

Schlicke, P. (1999), *Oxford Reader's Companion to Dickens*. Oxford: Oxford University Press.

Shattock, J. (1999), *The Cambridge Bibliography of English Literature*, Vol. 4. Cambridge: Cambridge University Press.

Slater, M. (1983), *Dickens and Women*. London: J.M. Dent and Sons Ltd.

Slater, M. (1999), *An Intelligent Person's Guide to Dickens*. London: Duckworth.

Slater, M. and Drew, J. (1994–2000), *The Dent Uniform Edition of Dickens' Journalism* (4 vols). London: J.M. Dent.

Smith, G. (1996), *Charles Dickens: A Literary Life*. Basingstoke: Macmillan Press Ltd.

Smith, G. (2003), *Dickens and the Dream of Cinema*. Manchester: Manchester University Press.

Stanley, A.P. (1893), *The Life and Correspondence of Thomas Arnold, D.D.* Minerva Library of Famous Books. London: Ward, Lock, Bowden and Co.

Sutherland, J.A. (2005), *Inside Bleak House*. London: Gerald Duckworth and Co. Ltd.

Thackeray, W.M. (1955), *Contributions to the Morning Chronicle*, ed. G.N. Ray. Urbana and London: University of Illinois Press.

Tillotson, G. and Hawes, D. (1968), *Thackeray: The Critical Heritage*. London: Routledge and Kegan Paul.

Tillotson, K. (1961) *Novels of the Eighteen Forties*. Oxford Paperback. London: Oxford University Press.

Tillotson, K. (1982) 'Introduction' to *Oliver Twist*. The World's Classics. Oxford and New York: Oxford University Press.

Trilling, L. (1953), 'Introduction' to *Little Dorrit*. New Oxford Illustrated Dickens. Oxford: Oxford University Press.

Wall, S. (1970), *Charles Dickens: A Critical Anthology*. Harmondsworth: Penguin Books Ltd.

Ward, A.W. (1882) *Dickens*. English Men of Letters. London: Macmillan and Co.

Williams, E. (1954), *Readings from Dickens*, introduced by Bernard Darwin. London: William Heinemann Ltd.

Wilson, E. (1961), *The Wound and the Bow*. University Paperbacks. London: Methuen.

Journals

Collins, P. (1993), 'The reception and status of the *Carol*'. *Dickensian*, 89, 170–6.

Cosnett, J. (2003), 'Charles Dickens – syndrome spotter: a review of some morbid observations'. *Dickensian*, 99, 22–31.

[Hamley, E.B.] (1857), 'Remonstrance with Dickens'. *Blackwood's Magazine*, 81, 490–503.

Hawes, D. (1972), 'Marryat and Dickens: a personal and literary relationship'. *Dickens Studies Annual*, 2, 39–68.

Lebrecht, N. (2005), 'Fagin with a new twist'. *Evening Standard*, 29 September 2005, 33.

Petrie, G. (2001), 'Silent film adaptations of Dickens'. *Dickensian*, 97, 7–21; 101–15; 197–213.

Stafford-Clark, N. (2005), 'The original soap opera and how it came to TV'. *Radio Times*, 22–28 October 2005, 14.

Index

This selective index includes critics, commentators, publishers, periodicals, members of the Dickens family and some of his fellow-writers. For adaptors of Dickens's works, dramatists, performers and other acquaintances, see Chapters 16, 18, 19 and 21.